Dear Father, Your Daughter Wants a Word With You

Stories, Revelations, and Honest Conversations with God

By: Terri Tuers

Dear Father, Your Daughter Wants a Word With You ---
Stories, Revelations, and Honest Conversations With God

Published by Terri Tuers/LuLu Publishing

All Scripture references in this book are taken from the New International Version of the Bible (NIV)

Ms. Tuers is available to speak at churches and conferences. To schedule an event contact her at Terri.tuers@yahoo.com

ISBN: 978-1-716-46676-2

DEDICATION

This book is dedicated to the Holy Trinity. To God the Father, who reveals Himself every day through our children and the experiences around us. To Jesus Christ, His beloved Son, and my personal Lord and Savior. And to the Holy Spirit, who is my daily inspiration, counselor, and my best editor.

To my three children, Rachel, Stephanie, and Greg, who have provided me with so much joy and many experiences to write about for an entire lifetime.

Lastly, to my dear husband, Rick, who encouraged me to finish this book and check off a major item on my "List of Unfinished Projects." He convinced me that this book was worth finishing.

"I found this book to be applicable, personal, and practical. In the midst of all that's happening in the world today, this book is a welcomed breath of fresh air. It is full of golden nuggets that brought my heart joy."

David Wagner
Founder
Fathers Heart Ministries
Franklin, TN

"I truly enjoyed Dear Father, Your Daughter Wants a Word With You. It was an enjoyable read, especially because I know Terri and her children. This is Terri's spiritual journey as a mother of two adopted daughters. Each chapter begins with an event in Terri's life, whether enjoyable or vexing. The difficulties and joys of parenting are followed by an honest conversation with God. This book exemplifies her trust and reliance on the Lord's help. It also reveals the awareness of the Father in her life. I found it to be realistic, thought provoking, relational, and faith enriching, especially for parents. For those reading this book, I pray that it would be an incentive to be more aware of the Father's place in their lives. May it bear much fruit in the lives of others."

Fr. George Brucker
Former Pastor of St. Paul the Apostle Church and Terri's Spiritual Advisor for 20 years
Albany, NY

CONTENTS

FINISHING A BOOK THAT WILL NEVER END

This book is comprised of real life stories from raising two daughters, Rachel and Stephanie. These stories will make you laugh and make you cry. I started journaling when they were babies. I wrote and meditated mostly when they were napping or late at night after they were asleep. When they became school age, I wrote while they were in school. My writings continued into their teen years and I wrote less frequently as they matured into adulthood. Each story is followed by a prayer to my Father.

One of the challenges of publishing this book was realizing that I am in the middle of a story that never ends. I used to ask myself, "When would be a good time to end it? After the girls' high school graduation? Or college graduation? Or after the first grandchild? Or after the last was born? The truth is, the story continues. As long as our adult children are alive, they are still our kids.

As our grandchildren grow, we continue to make memories with them. We continue to learn about ourselves, parenting, and the nature of God. Through writing this book, I have developed an insight into the heart of our heavenly Father. What a grace He has given me to learn more about Him. There is no end to my infinite Father, and so my education of heavenly things will continue until I meet Him face to face.

I hope that these writings and prayers will bless you, as much as they have blessed me. My hope is that you will begin to write about your own life. Each of us has a story to tell, especially of you are a parent. God wants you to learn more about Him. Ask the Father, and He will show you His character through the experiences you are having with your own children. The parenting years may seem long and never ending, but they are a treasure. The Father made us parents to change our nature and make us more like His Son, Jesus. Please don't miss this opportunity to learn more about yourself and your heavenly Father.

If you aren't a parent, don't worry. The Father still wants to reveal Himself to you. He wants you to draw closer to Him. He wants to be your first love. He wants you to realize how special you are to Him and how much He loves YOU. You may not hear that enough, or maybe you have never heard it, but God thought about you long before He made you. He has a very special plan and purpose for your life. His heart beats for you! Yes, YOU. Ask Him for ways that He wants to teach you about Himself, and He will. No matter your state in life, I pray that your eyes will be open to the wonders of our perfect parent, Daddy God, Abba, and Father. Through the stethoscope of this book, I hope you can hear the Father's heartbeat.

THE IMPORTANCE OF FATHERS

The family is the cell of society and the church. When a man engages God with passion, the society changes, and especially the family unit. It is documented that when a father is a passionate believer, there is a 75% to 95% likelihood that the children will also become passionate believers. If it's just mom, that percentage drops to about 15%.

When a man isn't engaged with God, it has a negative ripple effect on society and especially the family unit. It is estimated that 40% of homes in America today are fatherless. Of those that contain fathers, many dads are more engaged with work, other hobbies, and distractions of sports or social media.

Here are some alarming statistics from David Popenoe, the co-director of the National Marriage Project and sociology professor at Rutgers University. Popenoe is the author of the book, *"Life Without Father."*

-60% of America's rapists came from fatherless homes.

-72% of adolescent murderers grew up without a father.

-70% of long-term prison inmates are fatherless.

He continues: *"No one predicted this trend; few researchers or government agencies have monitored it; and it is not widely discussed, even today. But the decline of fatherhood is a major force behind many of the most disturbing problems that plague American society: crime; premature sexuality and out-of-wedlock births to teenagers; deteriorating educational achievement; depression, substance abuse and alienation among adolescents; and the growing number of women and children in poverty."*

For many people, their present well-being is directly correlated to their relationship with their father. For others, it's directly correlated to having an absent or abusive father. No matter what the father wound may look like, there is hope for healing as you turn to your heavenly Father.

What is Your Heavenly Father Like?

Having a heavenly Father may be a foreign concept to many people. How can we possibly have a relationship with a Father we cannot see or have never met? How can we have a relationship with a loving father in Heaven when our father here was so mean and abusive? Even the mere mention of "father" or "Happy Father's Day," can make many people cringe and run the other way.

No matter what your relationship is or was with your earthly father, I'm here to tell you that you have a Father in Heaven who is 100 percent perfect and loving in every way. How do I know this? In two ways. The first is through Scripture. The Bible paints a very clear picture of who our Father is. In the Old Testament, our Father is described as a potter who is constantly working to make us more like Him.

- Isaiah 64:8 *Yet you, Lord, are our Father. We are the clay; you are the potter; we are all the work of your hand.*

Our Father is steadfast. He never changes or leaves us. No matter what we do.

- Isaiah 63:16 "*Surely you are still our Father! Even if Abraham and Jacob would disown us, Lord, you would still be our Father. You are our Redeemer from ages past.*"

Throughout the New Testament, Jesus always refers to God as "Father." In fact, the Father and Son are one with the Holy Spirit. When God's divine plan was to save humankind, the Son became flesh and dwelled among us. It's a mystery of how Jesus was both man and divine. But Scripture testifies, over and over again, that when we see Jesus, we also see the Father.

- *John 10:30 "I and the Father are one."*
- John 6:46 "*No one has seen the Father except the one who is from God; only he has seen the Father.*"
- John 14:11 *"Believe me when I say that I am in the Father and the Father is in me; or at least believe on the evidence of the works themselves."*
- John 8:19 *"Then they asked Jesus, 'Where is your father?' You do not know me or my Father," Jesus replied. "If you knew me, you would know my Father also."*
- Matthew 23:9 *"And do not call anyone on earth 'father,' for you have one Father, and he is in heaven."*

What exactly is the Father like? In the New Testament, our Father is described as all loving. He's always ready to bless us. All we have to do is ask.

- Matthew 7:11 "*So if you sinful people know how to give good gifts to your children, how much more will your heavenly Father give good gifts to those who ask him?*"
- John 16:23 "*Jesus said, 'In that day you will no longer ask me anything. Very truly I tell you, my Father will give you whatever you ask in my name.'*"
- Psalm 103:13 "*As a father has compassion on his children, so the Lord has compassion on those who fear Him.*"

You don't need long, flowery prayers. You just come to the Father and share your heart. (Lamentations 2:19 – "Pour out your heart like water in the presence of the Lord." He already knows your needs, but He wants to hear from YOU.

- Matthew 6:8 "*Do not be like them, for your Father knows what you need before you ask Him.*"

St. Paul writes that God even adopted us as His children. He wants us to have an intimate, personal relationship with Him. He wants us to be so close that we would call Him Abba, which means Daddy or Papa.

- Romans 8:15 "*So, you have not received a spirit that makes you fearful slaves. Instead, you received God's Spirit when He adopted you as His own children. Now we call Him, 'Abba, Father.'*"

Our Father is merciful and forgiving. He wants us to be the same.

- Luke 6:36 "*Therefore be merciful as your Father is merciful.*"

- Matthew 6:15 *"But if you do not forgive others their sins, your Father will not forgive your sins."*

Just as an earthly parent disciplines their children, to make them better people, the Father also disciplines us. Often it comes in a form of a trial. In the Bible, the Father is often compared to a Master gardener, who prunes the plants to produce a higher yield and stronger plant. The Father doesn't prune us to be mean, but to cut away anything that keeps us from becoming more like His Son.

- Hebrews 12:17 *"Endure hardship as discipline; God is treating you as his children. For what children are not disciplined by their father?"*
- John 15:1 *"I am the true vine, and my Father is the gardener."*
- John 14:23 *"Jesus replied, 'Anyone who loves me will obey my teaching. My Father will love them, and We will come to them and make Our home with them.'"*
- John 15:10 *"If you keep My commands, you will remain in My love, just as I have kept My Father's commands and remain in His love."*

When Jesus' life was over, He ascended to Heaven to be with the Father. But He never left us as orphans. He gave us His Spirit, or Advocate, to teach, comfort, and remind us what Jesus taught, and convict us of sin. The Holy Spirit gives spiritual gifts, to those who are open to receive. The Father really has thought of everything to win us back to Heaven. First, He sent His son as a sin offering, and then gave us His Spirit, to assist us in our daily trials.

- John 15:26 *"When the Advocate comes, whom I will send to you from the Father—the Spirit of truth who goes out from the Father," said Jesus. "He will testify about Me."*
- John 16:28 *"I came from the Father and entered the world; now I am leaving the world and going back to the Father."*
- Luke 24:49 *"I am going to send you what my Father has promised; but stay in the city until you have been clothed with power from on high."*
- John 14:16 *"And I will ask the Father, and He will give you another advocate to help you and be with you forever."*
- Acts 2:33 *"Exalted to the right hand of God, He has received from the Father the promised Holy Spirit and has poured out what you now see and hear."*

MY RELATIONSHIP WITH THE FATHER

While knowing God as our father through Scripture is the first step, we can also know God, as father, through personal experience. After my dad died, when I was only 17 years old, I came to know God as my father as I observed how He took care of me and provided for my mom, grandma, and five siblings. I felt His comfort and presence as I journeyed through my rough college years, still grieving the loss of my earthly dad. Many times, when I prayed, I pictured myself crawling up onto Daddy God's lap, with His big, strong arms, holding me as I cried myself to sleep.

This image and presence of God was with me as I suffered the pain of infertility, the loss of many beloved dogs, and the loss of my mother. When I went through my divorce, Father God was the voice in my head, reassuring me of His love and provision as I struggled as a single mom. In Isaiah 54:6, I found a husband in God the Father: *"For your Creator will be your husband; the Lord of Heaven's Armies is His name!"* Wow! Who can compare with that?

The examples of how I experienced my heavenly Father can fill volumes. I am aware of His presence, leading me, loving me, disciplining me, and speaking to me every day. This book is actually an outgrowth of my personal relationship with the Father. He has enlightened my mind by showing me His qualities of parenting, by allowing me to experience the joys and sorrows of parenting.

I am so grateful that the Father gave me three children and six grandchildren to love. Our heavenly Father is relational. The more He shows me about His character, the more there is to learn. Through many experiences with my children, I have been able to think back to how my actions have impacted my heavenly Father. I pray that this book impacts you in the same way.

BEHIND THE SCENES OF WRITING THIS BOOK

I am the queen of unfinished projects. Just ask my husband or my kids. That's why this book, which I started 29 years ago, is now getting done. Like many of us, I make excuses of why I don't do certain things. *"I'm too busy. My kids and husband need me to do this or that. I'm having surgery. I'm recuperating. I have to clean and organize my house. I am going through a divorce. I have to go back to work full time. I've just added a full-time job to my part-time job. My dog is dying of cancer. My dog died, and I am grieving and don't feel like writing. I'm a single mom of a 10- and 13-year-old. My daughter is graduating from high school. Now college. Just started to date again. Now I'm engaged and planning a wedding. My other daughter is now graduating. We are buying a house and blending two families. I'm changing careers. I'm moving to Florida. And on, and on, and on."*

While there were many reasons why I didn't have the time to write, I realized that one of my biggest roadblocks was FEAR. This is a common thing among people when they venture into new territory. Each person has a different tolerance to risk and fear, but fear is one of our common denominators. People who know me know that I am a courageous person. I've always been a daredevil. I've walked into tense and dangerous ministry situations without blinking an eye. So, where did this fear come from? *"What if I'm a lousy storyteller and no one likes my work? What if I can't find a publisher? What if I find one and no one buys my book?"* These are all real conversations that crept into my brain for years. Every time I would try to write, these negative thoughts would whirl around in my head like a tornado.

I discovered that the source of my fear was believing the lies of the enemy (AKA the devil). It says in the Bible that Satan is the father of all lies. There is no truth in him. (John 8:44) So why didn't I realize this sooner? Why was I blind to the constant attack to prevent me from finishing this book? I guess my brain had a small opening for him to slip in. And slip in, and camp out, he did.

You see, when you are on an assignment from God, especially one that will bring the Father glory, the attacks from the other side are relentless and real. Satan's biggest lie of all was a collection of tormenting questions, which caused me to doubt (notice, I used the past tense here). *"What gives you the authority to write about God the Father, as if you know anything at all about Him? Who is actually going to believe that you hear God's voice? Who is going to accept what you have to say about the nature of the Father? Aren't there already too many Christian books on the market?"*

The answers, I have found, are really simple. I know Him because I seek Him. I know who He is because I read His Word. I can tell you about His nature because He speaks to me when I close off the noise of the world. I spend a lot of time with Him, asking questions and listening to the answers. I have access to His heart through my unshakeable faith in His Son, Jesus. I am a treasured child of the Father and what good Daddy wouldn't lavish gifts on His beloved?

Because I am God's kid, I can talk to Him about EVERYTHING. No subject is off limits: sex, money, marriage, parenting, friendship, temptations, addictions, death, loss, career decisions, people who are hard to forgive, disciplining children, you name it. The list is infinite. I love that when I ask Him questions, He answers me. He is available 24/7 and only wants the best for me. He loves me with an everlasting love. That I will never understand!

My relationship with my heavenly Father is unique because I am unique. So are you! Did you know that you are fearfully and wonderfully made? Your DNA and fingerprints do not match anyone on this planet. You are unlike any human He ever created in the past, present, or future. He has a distinctive purpose and plan for your life. He thought about you even before the foundations of the universe were made. He knows how many hairs you have on your head. He sees and hears you all the time and He wants an intimate relationship with you. Yes, you!

You, my dear reader, hear this today! The Father wants to have a tender relationship <u>with you</u>. Take that first step today. Ask Him to make Himself known to you, and He will. If you still doubt the very nature of God, I pray that this book will reveal delightful secrets about His nature. I hope you will discover Him. I pray that you will see God in a new light and draw close to Him. The Bible says, "Draw near to God and He will draw near to you." (James 4:8) He is waiting for you! I promise.

THIS IS MY STORY

Family Ties

I was born into a large Ukrainian Catholic family in Cleveland, Ohio. My mom had two brothers, lots of aunts and uncles, and cousins. My dad had four sisters and one brother. Each of his siblings had oodles of kids, which became my cousin connection. Our birthday parties always consisted of our immediate family and my huge tribe of cousins, or the "Cleveland Indians," as my grandma would call us. We were loud and fun, and we stuck together. When my grandpa died, grandma moved in with us. There were nine of us at every meal. My mom always said that cooking for us was like cooking for the Ukrainian Army. Even after we grew up, got married, and moved out, Mom still continued to cook for "her army."

In 1968, my dad had a major heart attack at home. Mom gave him CPR for almost 30 minutes, which is unheard of by today's standards. The ambulance brought him to the emergency room, which was only two miles from our house. Unfortunately, Dad was dead on arrival.

Then a miracle took place. Dad went to Heaven and the Lord asked him if he was ready to "come home." Just then, he said that all our faces scrolled by him, as if he were watching a filmstrip. When he said, "No, not yet," a force knocked him back into his body. It was the doctors who thought that they brought him back, but we found out otherwise. Dad lived to tell us about his encounter with the Lord in Heaven. He always said that he was living on 'borrowed time' and he wasn't afraid to die after this experience.

Five years later, his stressful day job, as well as his second job at night and on the weekends, took a toll on his health. On November 1, 1973, my father, who was only 44 years old at the time, had a coronary at work and died. My mom was left with six kids, ranging in age from five to 18. Although Dad had heart trouble since I was in the 7th grade, I never expected to lose him at such a young age. I was living two hours away as a college freshman and I never had the chance to say goodbye. Even if I had been near, it would not have mattered. Dad died before he reached the hospital.

Dad's death was a defining moment for me as well as the rest of the family. It was never the same in our house. Grandma cried all the time. My mom's substance abuse became evident and became more prominent. She even had two suicide attempts. I did not realize how sick she was at the time. The harsh words she had for me, such as "You are worthless" or "you are the biggest disappointment in my life," stuck to me like glue. Sadly, these jabs followed me into my adult life.

Mom's disease of addiction caused her to berate my sister, who was trying so hard to work and hold the family together. My four younger brothers acted out. They couldn't understand what was happening. Our once happy family was now a mess. Dad's passing had such a great impact on our entire family that all stories and time were marked by his death. The sadness and grief of losing a parent so young was profound. It weighed all of us down. I was angry with God for doing this to our family. I had to grow up quickly and become a caretaker for my mom, grandma, and my younger siblings. Sadly, I missed out on much of my childhood and young adulthood.

For almost 15 years following his death, I still did not have a good relationship with my heavenly Father. I was angry that my family was falling apart and believed that He didn't seem to care or help. The angrier I got, the more I blamed Him for my sadness and my wrecked nuclear family. My anger grew to the point that I was scared that He did not understand my feelings and that He would punish me.

Married Life

Two years after I graduated from college, I married a fellow I met at work in Erie, Pennsylvania. I moved to Albany, New York, right before we got married. I lived in Albany for most of my adult years until we moved to southwestern Florida in 2013.

My husband came from a large German-Irish family in Natrona Heights, Pennsylvania. He had a sister and two brothers. His brothers had a total of six children while his sister remained single. Both parents came from large, prolific Catholic families. At Thanksgiving, we gathered at his family gatherings where up to 60 people attended. As his cousins grew up, got married and had children, these celebrations would become more exciting with each passing year. Having a large ethnic family was in my DNA. It is what I knew and what I always wanted when I got married.

I was the first of six children in my family to get married. My brother, Joe, was second. Joe and his wife became pregnant within the first year of their marriage and had a baby boy, named Christopher. While I was happy for them, I couldn't help but wonder, "Why not me? Why not us?" My mom had certainly been fertile.

What? No Baby?

Imagine the shock and disappointment when after our first year of marriage, I wasn't pregnant yet. Well-meaning parents, siblings, in-laws and friends told me to "relax and stop thinking about it and then it would happen." But it never did. We went for tests. I tried many drug therapies. I had four surgeries, and still, no baby. Each holiday became a grim reminder of what we didn't have. I never expected to be infertile. I felt like a big failure since I couldn't produce a baby. The holidays became dreadful as I was surrounded by family and friends who had no trouble getting pregnant. Children were all around us. Everywhere but not in our home.

I was still angry at God for the loss of my dad. Why was God doing this to us? Was He punishing us? Was it because we had sex before marriage? Why wasn't my body working properly? Why did God give babies to everyone but us? What was He trying to teach us? All of this was happening during an era when infertility treatments and medications were not covered by insurance. It became a financial trial for us, as well an emotional one.

Early on, I thought that if we were meant to be parents, God would have allowed us to conceive. At one point, we just gave up and resolved to be a childfree couple. The medical merry-go-round of tests, drugs, and surgeries were too taxing, and so we quit. I was sure that I was never going to get pregnant, although I never lost hope.

During this time, we joined an infertility support group for childless couples, called "Resolve." We really needed the support of other couples who were going through the same thing. Unlike some couples in Resolve, who decided to remain child-free, we began to research adoption. Through months of counseling, I realized that it wasn't so much being pregnant that I was missing but becoming a mom. Pregnancy only lasts for nine months, while parenting lasts for a lifetime.

I will never forget the day we went to Catholic Charities to an adoption information meeting. A social worker told us the steps needed to adopt: the application process, a home study, three references from people who knew us well, and an actual home visit. They also prepared us for the cost, which we could pay in installments. Imagine getting a baby on layaway! I felt like we were buying a refrigerator at Sears. It was clinical and surreal at the same time. We even had a payment plan.

Since this was 1980, just seven years after Roe vs. Wade, we learned that babies were not plentiful for waiting couples. We were warned that it could take up to <u>three</u> years to adopt a healthy, Caucasian baby. If we wanted to adopt a "baby of color" or one with disabilities, there would be no waiting time. But we chose to wait.

More adversity. More waiting. More money. More scrutiny. More poking and prodding. It was clear that this process weeded out the ones who were not ready to become parents. Sometimes, couples would get a baby faster than they expected. This only happened if a couple dropped off the list for some reason. Usually, it was because they got pregnant. Since babies were so scarce, they only placed them in childless homes. We were praying that we would be one of those couples. But still, no baby.

Adoption was never my first option. I was not one-hundred percent comfortable with the idea, but I thought of it as an "insurance plan." It's always good to have insurance in case something bad happens. We would have a fall back option, not because something horrible happened, but because nothing happened. No pregnancy. No baby. So, what's the next best thing? On the outside, I was excited and willing to adopt. On the inside, I was filled with many fears and extreme sadness.

I had so many questions about adoption: How could I ever love a baby that I didn't carry in my womb? Would I be able to love someone else's child as much as our own? How long would it take us to bond with an adopted baby? What if the baby doesn't look like us? What if the birthparents change their minds and take the baby back? What if? What if? What if???? I was filled with doubt and fear throughout the entire process. Looking back years later, it is a wonder we adopted at all.

What Was God Doing?

My journey of faith, back in the 80s, was clearly not what it is today. My prayers were short and scattered. I felt like I was constantly in a storm and fighting with God. I thought that God was turning his back on us and was deaf to our cries at night. I was still angry with God for taking my dad in 1973, when I was only 17 years old. I didn't see these experiences as blessings to teach me about God's grace and provision. I just saw them as a rotten plot that God orchestrated to mess up my life plan, one that I so carefully planned since I was a little girl.

As my anger toward God increased, I stopped going to church. I stopped praying. I lived for myself. I was bitter at those couples around me that had children. One Christmas at Mass, I heard the priest talk about God's love for us and how He sent His only begotten Son to earth to show us the way back to the Father. I thought, "Yeah right. Why would anybody believe this? Why would we even want a relationship with such a harsh, punishing Father? What kind of parent was He anyway?" I really felt like God had forgotten me. (Psalm 22:1-20)

Being childless was really starting to get to me. I believe that the Father saw me at the end of my rope. Then one October night, in 1986, a miracle happened. In spite of all my doubts and fears, and in spite of all my unresolved anger toward God, we got a baby!

I will never forget the night that we found out. We were on our way back from Disney World. As we flew home, I told my husband that I never wanted to go back to Orlando, and especially Disney World, until we had a family. I was tired of seeing all these parents with strollers and kids in tow. When we arrived at home, the light on the answering machine was blinking. I listened to three or four messages before we came to "The Call."

"The Call"

I couldn't believe my ears! I screamed and called my husband. We listened to the message again and again. We couldn't believe that the agency actually had an 11-week-old baby girl for us. We cried and screamed. We hugged each other and called our social worker. Then we called our families. We went to the adoption agency the very next day to meet our baby girl.

When they handed her to me, I thought that I was dreaming. It seemed so surreal to be holding a baby. Our baby. She looked at me with trusting curious eyes. She grabbed onto my finger and put it in her mouth. She cried for a bottle and I fed her. She nuzzled into my neck as I gently burped her. We handed her back and forth while we decided on a name.

We named her Rachel, which we came to find out later, meant "lamb." The name Rachel also had other significance. The "Rachel Movement" was a group of women who gathered for healing, after having had an abortion. The name that we picked was just perfect for our little pro-life miracle, God's little lamb. We decided that Michele would be her middle name. Ironically, that was the name that her birthmother had chosen for her.

I stared into her beautiful face and thanked God for her birthmother, who chose life over an abortion. Rachel was absolutely perfect in every way. She had soft tan skin and large hazel eyes, like mine. She had brown fuzzy hair and a winning smile. She was very curious and attentive. She looked back and forth as we spoke to her. She didn't want to miss a thing. Sadly, we had to hand her back to the social worker that day. Her birthmother needed to say goodbye for the last time before the official placement and we needed to get ready to bring her home.

Even though we knew that we were on the approved adoption list, we thought it was bad luck to buy too many things for the baby. Plus, it was just impractical, since we had no idea of the sex, the age, or even the size of the baby until we received the call. The next 24-hours were a whirlwind of activity. We were still in shock that we were about to bring home our baby, even though we had been waiting for three years.

One of our first stops was at the one-hour photo shop. (Remember the days when you took pictures with a camera and then had the film developed? This was 1986.) We dropped off the roll of film, that documented our first meeting with baby Rachel, and went out for lunch. I was way too nervous and excited to eat. Just like a pregnant mother with morning sickness, I was in the bathroom half the time, getting sick. While my husband ate and our pictures were being developed, we used this hour to make a shopping list.

When we went to pick up our pictures, we stood there, pouring over each one. "Oh, isn't she adorable?" "Isn't she the MOST beautiful baby God ever created?" I could tell that the young male clerk had no patience for doting, new parents. When I showed him our pictures, he nonchalantly said, "If you've seen one baby you've seen them all." At this point, my husband grabbed my coat because I was ready to vault over the counter, like a mad woman. How could this kid talk about our new miracle like that? I was clearly post-partum hormonal.

I have met many people who take life and babies for granted. Unless you have experienced seven long years of infertility tests and adoption hoops to jump through, you will never know what it feels like to adopt. As we adjusted to life with a newly adopted baby girl, we were in awe of the little one that was entrusted to us. Life was busy and crazy, not just because we had a newborn and we were new parents, but because my husband was working full time and going to graduate school at night. I was managing a successful public relations/special events firm, complete with employees, clients, deadlines, and the pressure of making payroll. Before we got Rachel from Catholic Charities, I was already working 80 hours per week, running on adrenaline, coffee, and very little sleep. Without any immediate family near us, we quickly had to find childcare for when we were working and a babysitter for evenings and weekends.

Eventually, I sold my public relations/special events company, so I could stay at home full time and enjoy my daughter. I continued to work 40 hours per week at home for the advertising agency that bought my business. It almost seemed like a part-time job after working 80 hours per week. Those early weeks were tiring and stressful.

Our Second Adoption

Three years later, life began to even out as I became used to motherhood and working normal hours. We loved being parents so much that we longed to adopt again. We wanted to have a larger family and for Rachel to have a sibling. All during this time, we continued to pursue medical treatment for infertility. I have always been persistent (or stubborn according to some) and never gave up hope that I would get pregnant.

We interviewed local adoption attorneys and were met with many disappointments. We even thought of going to India, Korea, or Romania to adopt. One weekend, when I was at the end of my rope, we decided to go away and have my in-laws travel from Pittsburgh to watch Rachel. We needed some quiet time to talk about whether or not we wanted to adopt again, or just be content with one child. We decided that if we didn't have a baby in six months, we were going to totally stop everything. No more medical procedures, or answering ads, or calling lawyers, or meeting birthmothers.

When we arrived back home, we were given another great gift. My mother-in-law, who only saw a certain hairdresser twice a year when she came to visit, had an interesting conversation while we were away. When she went to get her hair done, the stylist asked if we were interested in adopting again because she had a customer, whose daughter was pregnant, and was looking for a good family. We couldn't believe this news! This clearly was an answer to our prayers. Shortly after this, we met the birthmother of our second child. In just three months from the time the stylist told my mother-in-law about this baby, we brought Stephanie home from the hospital. We were thrilled that the Lord met us and even shortened the time to adopt our second baby. We were blessed to know her birthmother while she was still carrying her, although we did not know it was going to be a girl at the time.

We were living the dream of being a family of four. I was reminded of the Scripture that said, *"Take delight in the Lord, and he will give you the desires of your heart." Psalm 37:4 (NIV)* We were so thrilled to bring Stephanie home! Although the circumstances of her adoption were extremely different, the emotions of joy, excitement, and awe were all the same. The day that she was born, we received "The Call" within minutes of her birth. Within hours, we were at the hospital, scrubbing and gowning up. It was surreal to hold our baby in the presence of her birth mom, who had just brought her into the world.

We named her Stephanie Patricia, after Stephen, my dad, who had passed away, and Patricia, who was my husband's sister that died of cancer at age 33. Both were strong, saintly people and we were sure that they could spend an eternity in Heaven helping our little Stephanie. Stephanie's homecoming from the hospital, at only 2-days old, was truly miraculous. Most couples had trouble adopting one baby, and here we had two. We shared our joy with Rachel, who was about to turn three, and Brenda, our lovable black Labrador.

The Meaning of "Yes"

Why did I begin this book with my family history? I wanted to set the stage for the thrill and awe of adoption. It was through our "yes" to become parents to two little girls, who originated from two separate families, that I began my journey back to God the Father. By having the unimaginable responsibility of raising our daughters, I was doubly blessed to learn so much about myself and about the nature of God, as our parent, our Daddy.

The emotions I felt toward the girls, in their various stages of development, were like a stethoscope against the heart of God. Many of the hilarious moments that I experienced as their mom, were just a twinkle of the laughter that God must have when parenting us. Many of the profound thoughts that I had, while observing the girls, were but a small glimpse into the mind of God.

The true miracle and blessing is that through the gift of parenthood by way of adoption, I grew closer to God the Father. My relationship with Him, which was fractured in 1973, when my dad died, was healed. I realized that the Father wasn't out to get me. I learned that He delights in me and that He never left my side during all the early trauma in my life. I discovered the many ways that the Father has provided, and will continue to provide, for me and my family. I learned to trust Him again.

I often thought of the couples that I met in doctors' offices, at adoption meetings, or at the Resolve Group who decided not to become parents. How were they doing years later with their choice? I can't imagine, even until this day, what my life would be like without Rachel and Stephanie.

You see, unlike getting pregnant "the old fashioned way," adoption is a choice. It is a huge decision and one that a couple does not take lightly. You don't adopt by accident. There are no "whoops" babies in adoption. Unlike a pregnancy, we could have opted out of the process at any time. If we changed our minds (and believe me, we went back and forth many times) we could have removed our names from the list. But we chose to say yes. While the order of events leading up to having a child is different in adoption, the rest is pretty much the same. Once you adopt, just like giving birth, there is no turning back. You become parents forever.

The Amazing Truth

We are all adopted sons and daughters of God the Most High. In Scripture, Paul talks about adoption to the churches at Ephesus (Ephesians 1:5), Rome (Romans 9:4), and Galatia (Galatians 4:5). Paul wanted them to understand that adoption was clearly God's idea. God wanted us all to be a part of His family, with all the rights of benefits of being born into the family. At any point in creation history, don't you think that God could have stopped after creating the seas? Or after the fish? Or the mammals? No! Just like we weren't content to be a childless couple, God was not content being childless either. Just like we yearned for a baby, so did God. Just like we felt like something very special was missing from our lives, so did God. And so, He made all of us!

The miracle story gets even better. When Adam and Eve sinned in the Garden of Eden, our relationship with God was severed. Sin and death entered the world. The plan of God to be in perfect communion with man was foiled after the fall of Adam and Eve. He had to be so sad and angry at the same time.

I know I have experienced just a small taste of this sadness and anger each time one of our children severed their relationship with us. At different times in their lives, all three children have stopped talking to us or seeing us. For one child, it was a couple of weeks. Another it was for several months. And another it was six years! In spite of our valiant effort to win each of them back into relationship with us, nothing worked. As hard as we tried, it was impossible for us to do anything to make it right again. They had to decide to come back.

In the case of the fall of Adam and Eve, there was something the Father could do to restore a relationship His children. His plan was to send His only Son, Jesus, to earth to become one of us and to show us the way to Heaven. He created a bridge to the Father by paying an extreme price for all our sins, once and for all. Our acceptance of Jesus and what He did on the cross has allowed us to share in His Divine life here on earth and forever in Heaven. What a miracle. He wanted all of His "adopted" kids to make it home around His Heavenly dinner table. Amazing love!

Through the gift of parenting my daughters, I have received the grace of having profound moments of insight into the mind and of heart of God. I do not believe that I ever would have had this if I had not become a parent. I know that I would have had a very different understanding of the Father if we had chosen to be childless. Who knows? My anger and severed relationship could have continued for many more years. I am forever grateful that we did adopt two beautiful daughters.

Second Marriage

When Rachel was 13 and Stephanie was 10, their dad and I became separated and then divorced. Five years later, I remarried. My husband, Rick, had a son, Greg, from his previous marriage. I always wanted a boy and was thrilled when I finally had a son. While those early years were hard on everyone, especially the three kids, I am happy to say that after much prayer, counseling, and patience, we finally have a blended family that works. It certainly took a lot of time and compromise. We give all the credit for our new family to the Lord!

In 2011, we started another season in our life. I took an early retirement because of an illness and started my own company, which included writing educational curriculum, teaching, and publishing. In 2012, Rick retired after 31 years with the state of New York. We sold our family home in Albany, New York and moved into a 2-bedroom apartment, while we looked for a place in Florida. We found a beautiful development in May, 2013, and moved seven months later. Today, we continue to be full-time residents of the Sunshine State.

Grandparenting - Act 2

I am now a proud grandmother of six grandchildren. Life slows down a bit for grandparents. When I became a new mom, I was ill prepared for the task before me. Babies don't come from the agency or the hospital with an "owner's manual." I was so afraid of doing something wrong. I feared that any mistake we made would scar our daughters for life.

In a sense, I felt like parenting my own children was like Act 1 of a very long play. Each phase seemed like it would go on forever. There were many days when I was tired and longed for an intermission. Unlike plays with many rehearsals and even a dress rehearsal, there were no rehearsals for parenting. It was truly like a live play.

There are no "rewinds" or "do overs." As they say in Hollywood, "the show must go on." Life certainly is not a dress rehearsal, and neither is parenting. We only get one chance at each day. In hindsight, from my seat at their college graduations, life had skipped by like a blink of an eye.

While parenting it is much like being in a long play with no intermissions, we do get an intermission when we become grandparents. Before the final curtain call and bow, the Father has blessed me with another glimpse of His everlasting love by giving us grandchildren. Thanks to God's abundant grace, we pray that we will live to see our great-grandchildren. That's up to Him. For now, we are enjoying this tremendous treasure.

Meet the Grandchildren

Our oldest grand-daughter, Gwen, was born in 2007. What a gift she is to our family. Because she was our very first grandchild, there is a bond that we share that is hard to describe. We were present when she was born and fell in love with her immediately, like we have with all of our grandchildren. As I observe Gwen and spend time with her, she clearly has her own personality, talents, and mannerisms. She reminds me that God is so creative, always making each human unique. We also have a beautiful granddaughter, Charlotte, who was born on my birthday in

2013. We didn't meet her until January 2016 (more on this later). Gwen and Charlotte belong to our oldest daughter, Rachel. I love to watch and listen to Charlotte. At her young age, she is wise beyond her years, inquisitive and smart. She can also revert back to being a baby at a moment's notice.

We have two beautiful grandsons by our daughter, Stephanie. Daniel was born in 2014 and Owen was born in 2017. They are both little treasures. We never thought Stephanie could conceive because of a medical issue, so we were blessed when she did. Imagine our surprise and joy when she gave birth to two baby boys! I was fortunate to be present at both of their births. Daniel has the energy of the Energizer Bunny. His smile and radiant blue eyes melt the hearts of all who meet him. Owen is a cutie who looks much like Stephanie when they were the same age. It's delightful to see Owen interact with his big brother, Daniel. I hope that this loving bond continues.

Our son, Greg, and his wife, Xu, are the proud parents of Stone and Sloan. Stone and his sister are only 18 months apart. Stone was born in 2017 and Sloan was born in 2018. Both of them are joyful, athletic, smart, and bi-lingual in Chinese and English. Greg and Xu have very busy lives working full-time and parenting two in diapers. When we watch how they interact with their adorable kids, we are reminded of why God gives babies to the young! I envy their energy.

THE EARLY YEARS

LETTERS FROM 30 YEARS AGO
From infancy to toddlers to elementary school

After many years of infertility treatments, we finally decided to adopt. These years were marked with busyness. When we got the call that our first child, Rachel, was joining our family, I had a public relations/special events business to run. I had employees and clients who depended on me. My husband was working full time and often traveled with his job. He was also taking two courses each semester to compete his M.B.A. During these years, I sold my company to become a full-time mom. What a big adjustment! This was a time of spiritual growth, where I became more conscious of the Lord, and how He wanted a personal relationship with me. I am thankful for the two Christian mothers' groups I belonged to, a supportive pastor, and the members of our Holy Family prayer group.

Baby Oh Baby!

I will never forget the day we brought Rachel home. We still had a hard time believing that we were parents, and yet, here was this gorgeous, 11-week old baby girl. She looked at us with trusting eyes and smiled. Little did she know that we had no idea what we were doing. Her daddy was the youngest of three children and had zero babysitting experience. I was the second oldest of six children and took care of my four younger brothers. I also made money babysitting in middle and high school.

I quickly learned that this was so different from babysitting. We were in charge! What responsibility we had for everything. Her foster mom wrote out a "schedule" for taking care of her. After all, she was with her for the last 11 weeks. I thought, "this was a piece of cake." This baby came with directions. How silly of me to think that our 11-week-old baby could read this schedule.

Rachel did not follow the foster mom's schedule at all. The things that used to soothe her when she was crying didn't work at all. We were truly pioneering the rough road of parenting. I prayed more than ever during the first few weeks of becoming a parent. I asked God for wisdom to know what to do with an infant. I asked for supernatural strength to get through the day on very little sleep. I asked for grace to receive all the advice that people were giving me about being a mother. I asked for provision for my company, as I learned that we needed to find new office space and move within a month of bringing Rachel home. I asked for tolerance for my family, who would say things like, "An adopted daughter! How nice. But don't worry, someday you will have a real child of your own."

Dear Father,

I am overwhelmed by this great gift you have given me! Help me to know how to be a good mother. Help me learn how to juggle the responsibilities of being a mom and a wife. I thank you that whenever I call on You, You are right there to answer my cry. You are a good, good Father.

What Is Heaven?

Saturday morning cartoons. What an American custom! I often watch them with the girls, and I am amazed at what the commercials pressure you to buy: every toy under the sun, popular games and electronics, and happy meals at fast food chains. Every once in a while, there is a more serious public service announcement denouncing drugs and alcohol or warning kids not to talk to strangers.

Before I became a parent, I worked in advertising. I never realized how much companies pressure people to have, buy, and own things. When I was growing up in the 60s and 70s, most people were defined by what they believed in. Now it seems that the culture has drastically shifted to identify people by what they own.

As a parent, I struggle to downplay the material side of life and play up the side of storing up Heavenly treasures. We had a little victory the other day. I was talking to Rachel about Heaven and all the things I was looking forward to when I got there. I shared first. "First and foremost, Father, I look forward to seeing You face-to-face and just being in Your presence." I realized that this was a bit abstract for a 5-year-old. Then I got a little silly with her. Here's what I hope that heaven will be like. Heaven is where you can eat all the chocolate you want and not get a migraine headache or gain a pound. Heaven is where I will be able to visit with friends and family for an eternity, especially the ones I haven't seen due to death, geography, or the daily pressures and circumstances of earthly life. I am so busy being a wife and mother, I regret that I don't have time to play my oboe anymore or make reeds. But in Heaven, I look forward to playing in the Heavenly orchestra, giving all the glory and praise to the Lord, without ever getting tired or breaking a reed.

Heaven is where we will be able to swim, surf, and play in the sun without getting too hot or sunburned. The water will always be the perfect temperature and we will never fear drowning or getting bitten by a shark. In Heaven, we will be able to go downhill skiing without falling or getting too cold, or risk breaking an arm or leg.

In Heaven, I will never be at a loss in my prayer time. I look forward to a reunion with Mary, Jesus' mom. I have talked to her so much in this life, I feel like we are old friends already. I can't wait to meet my patron saint Therese of Lisieux, also known as the Little Flower. I wonder what it will be like to talk to Clare and Francis of Assisi, Kateri, Anthony of Padua, and even Ann, Jesus' grandmother. I wonder what Joseph, Jesus' earthly dad, looks like? Does he really help people on earth sell their houses (an old Catholic wives' tale)? And Joan of Arc -- there's a brave one I can't wait to meet. The Apostles, who followed Jesus and started the first church and died for their faith, will be waiting there too. I wonder what St. Peter is like? Does St. Michael the Archangel have really big wings? I look forward to a reunion with all my heroes in Heaven!

As I shared some of my thoughts on Heaven with Rachel, I asked her to imagine what Heaven is like in her mind. She said that Heaven is where she can sit on Jesus' lap and read stories. In Heaven, she will be able to play with Brenda, our black Labrador, who died in December 1991. Rachel looks forward to getting any toy she wants just by wishing for it. Imagine that! Her mom won't be saying, "You don't really need that, or we can't afford that." In Heaven, Rachel looks forward to swimming all day and not having to do chores or go to school. She anticipates riding on all the amusement park rides as many times as she wants, with no long lines or feeling sick after the roller coaster.

Dear Father,
I truly believe that "eye has not seen or mind cannot even imagine" the wonders you are preparing for those who keep Your commandments and accept your Son, Jesus, as Lord and Savior. Help us to prepare for the day when we will fully share in the Kingdom. Help us to keep our eyes fixed on spiritual things, not earthly things which will pass away. Thank you for the grace of knowing that whatever we surrender in this life, to serve You, will be repaid a thousand fold in the next life.

PS. I am <u>really</u> looking forward to seeing you!

True Thanksgiving

It says in the Old and New Testament Scriptures that we should constantly give thanks. Give thanks for everything. I have been trying to keep this commandment with our children. In our prayer time, we always begin with, "Thank you, God, for ______" and they fill in the blank. It's amazing what the kids come up with. At ages two and five, their prayers are so sweet and innocent. "Thank you, God, for my home, my family, my school, my cat, for bringing Daddy home safely from the business trip, for not being poor, for our vacation, for my room, for my toys, etc." These are all things that are important to children up to age five. The funniest ending is when Stephanie (age two at the time) says, "Thank you, God, for candy" after every prayer! You know, she is right.

I now realize that every good thing, down to candy, is a gift from God. Everything we own belongs to God. It's His gift to us. We are only stewards of this property, including our land. We never could have acquired this on our own, although I do know people who think that God had nothing to do with it. But I believe that everything of goodness comes from above.

Dear Father,

Thank you for the blessing that the children are to me. Thank you for their simplicity and the wisdom that comes from their mouths. Thank you for using them to teach me that everything, no matter how small or mundane, comes from You. I can't thank You enough, Father, for all you have given me throughout my entire life. Help me to always have the attitude of gratitude.

Bonding

I remember one night when Stephanie was three, we were cuddling and reading a bedtime story. She looked up at me with her beautiful green eyes and sweet smile. She cuddled closer and said, "Mommy, I never want to leave you." My heart melted!

I remember the times I believed that I might not bond with "someone else's child," a child that I did not give birth to. Looking back, I realized how ridiculous that fear was. This fear was planted when I believed the lie that you could never love a child that you didn't birth.

After we adopted each of our daughters, the Lord gave me many opportunities to forgive others. People would say things like: "Someday you <u>will</u> have a child of your own." These girls ARE my own! All children are on loan from the Lord and adoption grafts them into a family forever. Yes, their birthmothers brought them into the world, but their dad and I had the privilege of raising them. Some people would ask us questions about their "real mother." What was I? The "unreal mother?" The overwhelming love we had for them made our children "our own." I bonded to them as if I had have given them birth. Adopting them into our family made them heirs to all that was ours. They are our legacy. They are permanent leaves on our family tree. They have our last name. These blessings flow from God to adoptive parents.

Dear Father,

When Stephanie cuddled and said that she never wants to leave me, My heart skipped a beat. This is exactly how I feel about You. During so many sad and hard times, I can visualize sitting on Your lap, with Your big strong arms around me, and my head leaning against Your chest. I never want to leave that safe place. The love that radiates from You, even in my thoughts, warms my heart and covers me like a down comforter. Thank you for allowing me to feel Your love in this way. Thank you for my two adopted daughters and the tremendous bonding I have felt towards them since the very beginning. They truly are MY OWN.

Fear

I was the second oldest of six kids. I had a lot of responsibility from a very young age. My youngest brothers are 10 years younger than me. I used to change their diapers and feed them. I also spent years babysitting other children. On the day we brought our first adopted daughter, Rachel, home from the adoption agency, I was gripped with fear. Suddenly, I forgot how to do everything. My husband was even worse. He was the youngest child of three and never had younger siblings to watch. He had zero baby experience.

I quickly realized that it's one thing to watch other children and a completely different scenario when the baby is your own. Rachel was 11 weeks-old when we brought her home. Prior to her homecoming, she was taken care of by a great couple in a foster home. Thankfully, she was already sleeping through the night, which made a big difference.

It was a huge adjustment for the both of us. Besides crazy work schedules and graduate school, we were used to coming and going as we pleased. We only had a dog, who was like our first baby. It didn't take me very long until I felt overwhelmed with the responsibility of being a mom and a company president.

Three years later, when we adopted our second daughter, Stephanie, she was only two days old. The challenges were completely different. As a newborn, I was up every few hours for feedings. By the time Rachel and my husband got up, I just wanted to stay in bed and sleep. I quickly discovered that having two kids was exponentially more difficult than one. I never had help with either baby since both of our families lived 500 miles away.

In my quiet time, which was rare, I would express my fears to God. I wanted to do the best for my kids, but I was feeling so inadequate. In addition to these present fears, I was also afraid for what was ahead. How was I going to tell them that they were adopted? How would they react to their adoption stories? I loved them so much and I was afraid that I was going to do something to mess them up. Isn't that one of a parent's worst fears?

The consolation and wisdom I received during these times came directly from God's love letter to us, the Bible. In Proverbs 4:11-13, it says: *"I will teach you wisdom's ways and lead you in straight paths. When you walk, you won't be held back; when you run, you will not stumble. Take hold of my instructions; don't let them go. Guard them, for they are a key to life."*

Dear Father,
Thank you that your Word has all the answers I will ever need for any situation in my life. Thank you for providing your wisdom in loving, practical ways. Thank you for calming my fears and giving me the faith to believe in myself. I am comforted that you said, "I will never leave you nor forsake you. I am with you always, even until the end of time." With these amazing promises, why should I be afraid of anything?

Forgiveness

Why does it take adults so long to work out our differences? Why do we take days, or weeks, to think about what "so and so" said or did? Why do we obsess over one another's motives or hidden agendas? What a waste of time.

When I watch Rachel and Stephanie interact with their friends, they have arguments too. As young as they are, even pre-school age, they experience personality clashes. But it doesn't take them days or weeks to resolve their differences. I've seen it only take minutes. Each voices their own opinion, they negotiate what they want or need, and they are quick to apologize. Why can't we "big people" be more like these "little people?" I have a lot to learn from my little children.

Dear Father,

Help me to be more childlike, not childish, in my approach to resolving differences with family or friends. Help me to be more accepting of others, more forgiving, and more "little." As it says in the Bible: "People were also bringing babies to Jesus for him to place his hands on them. When the disciples saw this, they rebuked them. But Jesus called the children to Him and said, 'Let the little children come to me, and do not hinder them, for the kingdom of God belongs to such as these. Truly I tell you, anyone who will not receive the kingdom of God like a little child will never enter it.'" Luke 18:15-17

Loving the Unlovable

Every family seems to have at least one "black sheep," and if you don't know who it is, it's probably you. You know the type. They usually have "some history" which makes interacting with them challenging. I saw this at family reunions, funerals, and weddings. When the "black sheep" arrived, all of a sudden, it got quiet. People in the family repositioned themselves to make ignoring this person easier.

When my grandfather died, our family traveled to be at his funeral in Cleveland. Rachel was only two and one-half at the time. I will never forget when my uncle (the black sheep) entered the funeral home. People started to fidget and talk softly. Rachel, in her loving way, ran up to my uncle to say hi. He picked her up and she kissed him on the cheek. He hugged her for over five minutes. I went over to say hello and asked if Rachel was being "too loving." My uncle warmed up to me and said, "No. Rachel was just fine." When I stepped back and thought about this interaction, I felt shame and guilt over not being more loving and accepting of this man. Why did I wait to go up to him and welcome him to his dad's funeral? I don't know how this interaction affected the rest of the family, but it affected me with a deep conviction of repentance.

Dear Father,
I repent of all the times I failed to show love. Sometimes my pride or my memory of keeping wrongs, gets in my way. Thank you that you had to show me this side of myself, through my kind and innocent daughter. Make me more childlike, Father, so I can love others like You love me. I thank you, Father, that there are no "black sheep" in your family.

Divorce

This week my husband travelled to Europe on business. He had been away for business before, but never for that long. He also never travelled that far. Communicating between so many time zones was a first for our family. Around the sixth day without Daddy, we were in the car heading to the store. Rachel, our five-year-old said, "If this is what it's like to be a kid in a divorced home, then I want no part of it."

I almost drove off the road! I was so amazed by her perception of what single-parent living must be like for a child: The same old Mom spends every waking minute with you except for the time away in Kindergarten. What a drag." This reinforced my belief that children want and need love and support from both parents, for optimum growth and development.

Dear Father,
Bless all marriages and families. Help parents of young children to work together to love and support them in their developing years. Give extra grace to the men and women who are going through a separation or divorce. Guide them to always think of the children first, the children's needs and making them feel secure. Bless all single-parent homes and give these moms and dads the energy and courage to raise the children entrusted to them, even when circumstances at home are not the best.

Chatter Box

Both of my girls were so happy when they began to talk. They started with sounds, then words, then phrases, and then complete sentences. When they were infants, I told my husband that I could not wait for each of them to start talking. Be careful what you wish for.

I believe that each girl, Stephanie and Rachel, were learning the ropes of being female, even before they could talk. Females speak about 20,000 words a day, while males only speak 7,000. They made up time by talking to me non-stop from the moment they got up until bedtime.

When we were in the car, I loved to listen to what they had to say. One of their cutest observations were dozens of birds on utility lines in the winter. "Mom, why are there so many birds up there? What are they doing? Do they ever get bored? Where is their house? Don't you think they are cold up there? Don't you think they should be home? What do they eat in the winter? If there is electricity running through the wires, why don't their little feet get burned?" I was getting tired of all the questions and trying to come up with answers.

They never liked the answer, "I don't know," so I used to make things up. When driving through the country, we saw miles and miles of hay bales, all rolled up and wrapped in white plastic. "What are those, Mom?" "Why Stephanie, it's a marshmallow farm." I think she believed that one until she got into middle school.

My days as a mother of two daughters, under the age of five, were filled with listening to them talk. Most of the time, it was repetitive and mundane. Sometimes I wanted to duct tape their mouths shut, just to enjoy a few hours of peace and quiet. And then I thought of my Father in Heaven, who is so patient and kind. He never closes His ears to our communication. How gracious He is.

Dear Father,
You never grow tired of hearing us talk to You. Even when we pray the same things, day after day, You still listen. The fact that You maintain a personal relationship with EACH ONE of us just boggles my mind. I pray constantly and you never shut me out. I also listen to Your voice for guidance, wisdom, comfort, and peace. How You manage to keep all this straight with over 7 billion people in the world, speaks volumes to me of Your power and greatness. Thank you for being a patient, understanding Father, who is available 24/7.

My Head in the Clouds

When I was raising my girls, we didn't have cell phones and tablets to distract them from wanting to play outside. As a stay-at-home mom, we were living on a very limited income and so we took advantage of many free activities. We had so much fun playing outside that our home became a magnet in the neighborhood for other children. One afternoon after lunch, I looked out of my kitchen window, and there were 14 kids in our backyard. A favorite pastime was to spread a blanket on the grass and watch the clouds. The game we played was called "What do you see?" As we watched the clouds, everyone took a turn to say what they were seeing. We saw mountains, fish, bears, flowers, a sword, and more. What a great way to slow down, be creative, and marvel at God's handiwork.

Today, with all the hustle and bustle of life, I don't see many parents (my adult children included) slowing down to have fun, creative, unstructured time with their children. They drive their kids from one activity to another with little free time in the week. Children benefit from creative play and unstructured time. Adults do too. Sometimes I am guilty of not slowing down enough to look at the clouds.

Dear Father,

Help me to remember these precious moments of my daughters' childhood and slow down. When I do, I can really feel Your presence. Help the young parents around me learn the value of slowing down and observing your marvelous creation with their kids.

Angels and Childlike Faith

I read to my girls every day, and not just at bedtime. One of my favorite books was a collection about angels. Some were Scriptures from the Bible and others were actual stories where people encountered an angel. I was as fascinated as the girls when we read about real-life encounters with angelic beings. When they were between three and six years old, I was amazed at their childlike faith. They never questioned the Scriptures or the stories. They just believed. I marvel at how different children are than adults, especially when it comes to faith. Children are so quick to believe and trust. Why can't I be more like them?

Dear Father,

It says in your Word that unless we become as little children, we will not enter the kingdom of Heaven. Now I know why. It pleases You when we have 100%, rock solid, unwavering faith in You. You delight in our trust that You will always take care of us. We never have to worry as long as we are in relationship with You. Help my unbelief and strengthen my faith each and every day. You are my everlasting Father, and I am your little girl.

Kids Say the Darndest Things

We were practicing Catholics when our girls were born, and so many of these stories reflect some Catholic things we used to do. Children are like parrots. They repeat everything we say -- some good and some bad. Sometimes they even put their own twist on what they have heard me say or things they have observed. One day, I walked into Rachel's bedroom and she was yelling at her baby sister. Stephanie had crawled into her sister's room and got into her bottom desk drawer. There, she found a rosary and started to swing it around like a wild west lasso. Rachel yelled, "Stop that! You're going to shake the holy out of the rosary!" I cracked up.

When Catholics enter a church, they dip their fingers into a holy water font, which is usually attached to the wall by each entrance of the church. Then they bless themselves by making the Sign of the Cross. Stephanie, when she was only two years old, used to walk by the dog dish in the kitchen, dip her hand in the dog's water bowl and bless herself.

When Stephanie was sick with a high fever, and we were waiting to take her to the doctor's office, Rachel got out my bottle of holy water and prayed that she would be healed. Stephanie also blessed us with holy water, as she had seen the priest do at church, only she got the names of the Trinity wrong. "In the name of the Father, the Son, and the hole in my head, Amen."

Dear Father,

I never laughed so hard as when she added a new person to the Trinity! Thank you for giving me these children. They may keep me hopping, but they also keep me laughing all the time. My only question is, do You laugh at us too?

Humorous Times

I just love my children's perception of life. There is so much humor present if we don't take life too seriously. When Rachel was only four, we took her to a family funeral. The family was understandably grieved and the brief service in the chapel of the cemetery was solemn. At a moment when the priest paused for a silent prayer, Rachel looked up and said, "Look Mommy! Jesus has boobies." She pointed to a stained glass window behind the priest and sure enough, His chest was exposed. This made everyone laugh! By this point, we all needed a lighter moment. Your promise came true. Blessed are those who are sorrowing for they shall be comforted. Children's humor is one of many ways that You console us.

A few years later, our college friends, lost their seven-year old son, Brian, to Leukemia. I will never forget how sad and tense the atmosphere was in the funeral home at that wake. In walked Brian's dad, Joe, with his wife and five-year old son, Scott. Joe was trying to prepare Scott for this experience and wanted to make sure that Scott knew that his brother, Brian, was really in Heaven. As they went to the coffin, you could hear Joe whisper. "Scott, remember, it looks like Brian is sleeping, but he's not really sleeping. I mean he's not going to wake up here anymore. It just looks like he's sleeping. He's really in Heaven, though."

Scott absorbed all of his dad's words. He slowly walked up to the coffin of his big brother, got up on the kneeler to get a better look, and just gazed at Brian. He was quiet for a long time. Then his dad leaned down to him and whispered, "How are you doing? Do you have any questions?" Scott said he was fine, and he only had one question.

Everyone in the funeral home seemed to lean in to hear the one big question of this adorable five-year old. "If Brian really isn't sleeping, then why is everyone whispering?" Thank you, Father, for the comic relief.

Dear Daddy God,
Thank you for the gift of humor. Thank you that it helps me to see the lighter side of every "bad" experience in my life. Thank you for reminding me that you are always with me, even in the bad times. I am grateful that when I stay in constant contact with You, there really are not any "bad times."

Lesson of the Lightning Bug

When my girls, Rachel and Stephanie, were little, we used to go outside at night and collect lightning bugs. They were fascinated that a little bug had “a light inside.” I gave them each a jar with holes punched in the lid for air. They would add grass and other little bugs for the bigger bugs to eat. They would stare at these bugs for hours. I thought it was amazing that they were drawn to light. Just like the summer bugs that found their way into their room from a crack in the screen, aren’t we all drawn to light?

When I prayed today, I saw the world nearly in total darkness. There were many small dots of light and in some places, several bright dots burned together. This vision of the world did not look like the NASA map I was used to, where the countries that had electricity were illuminated. In the NASA map, vast sections of Africa, South America, and Asia were mostly in darkness because they didn't have electricity. However, large, more developed sections of these continents were lit up.

I asked the Father what this all meant. Why was I being shown the world map in darkness? The answer was: “This is what I see from Heaven. The small dots of light are praying individuals, praying couples and families, prayer groups in the home, Houses of Prayer, and real praying churches.” Where many gather together to pray and worship the Lord, there is a light.

I was perplexed at this since I know that there are <u>many</u> churches here in America. We also saw many churches when we traveled recently to Europe. Yet these areas were still in a lot of darkness. Not all churches are true houses of prayer, unfortunately. They may gather together for Sunday worship, but their hearts are far from the Lord. Many priests and ministers have also grown lukewarm. Many are preaching what people want to hear instead of the authentic Gospel of Jesus Christ.

The Holy Spirit wants to fan the flame of faith around the world and bring the churches back to their central purpose: to worship the Lord Jesus Christ, to take care of widows and orphans, to make disciples of all nations, and to support the missionaries who travel to foreign lands to spread the gospel. It's time to move from darkness into the wonderful light of Christ.

Dear Father,
I am sorry that I have not always been a bright light burning for You. There have been times that I have even fallen so far from You. But in Your mercy, You have welcomed me back, given me a robe, and put a ring on my finger. Lord, deepen my faith and my prayer life. Thank you, Father, that You have used my children to teach me about the fascination with light through observing the simple lightning bug. Someone once said, that if You could put a light in the butt of an insect, just imagine what You could do with us! Mold us and make us be a light that burns brightly for You. Let the light of Christ, Your Son, draw others into a relationship with You, so that everyone you send to us may be saved.

Be More Child-like

Having two daughters has been the greatest blessing to me. Before I had children, I never slowed down enough to observe the nature of children. Their curiosity. Their joy in the simple things. Their trust in parents to handle everything. They believe that parents or guardians will always provide for their every need. They have unshakable confidence in parental wisdom to know the answers to questions like "do fish get married?" "How long do horses sleep every night?" "What makes a cake rise?" "Why don't we ever see fat monkeys?" "If humans are superior to animals, how could that woman on TV leave her newborn in a dumpster?"

The greatest gift of having children is similar to having a front row seat to learn what it means to be child-like. Because Jesus said in Scripture that "unless you become like a child you will not enter the kingdom of Heaven," I needed to study what that meant. Jesus yelled at the apostles when the children came to Him and they tried to push them away. "The kingdom of Heaven belongs to such as these." Children don't have all the answers and so they look to us for help. They cannot provide for themselves, so they trust that we will. They need constant teaching and affirmation to grow into the person that they were created to be.

Dear Father,

Let my prayer always be to "never let me forget that I am your child, dearly loved and cherished. Help me always to come to You with child-like faith and confidence that You are my Daddy. There is nothing to fear for You are always with me.

Raising Guide Dogs

When Rachel was five and Stephanie was two, we applied to be a foster home for seeing eye dog puppies. I thought that this would be a good experience for the girls and our family. I was a stay-at-home mom at the time, and I could devote a lot of energy into puppy raising. We applied and two weeks later, we were accepted by Guiding Eyes for the Blind (based in Yorktown Heights, NY). Shortly after that, we received our first pup, Sibley. She was an adorable black Labrador, and it didn't take long for us to bond with her.

We were referred to as "puppy raisers" and we had an important job to do. Raising a guide dog was an 18 to 24-month process. After a pup passed its first set of tests at the breeding center, they were placed in a home at seven to eight weeks old. And then we began to train them. We attended training meetings every other week. Each quarter, we met with a director from the main school for a "puppy evaluation." The girls loved these meetings, but I was a wreck. They girls saw this like a getting a report card, and I did too. Being an overachiever, I always wanted straight As.

After 18 months of training and socializing the dog, they had to be surrendered to the school. When they arrived back at school, they would go through a vet exam and extensive testing to see if they would advance to the next level of training. If a dog made it to this level, they were placed with a blind client. The client and his dog roomed together at the school for three weeks. During this time, they both received intensive training.

When the time came to "let go," and surrender the pup back to the headquarters, the school gave us a week or two notice. This gave us adequate time (or so they thought) to prepare us to say goodbye. I will never forget the day I got the news about surrendering Sibley. We loved her so much, and the girls were bonded beyond description. As young as they were, they helped to take care and train our pup. I was at the bank when I got "the call" that we had to turn her in. I was so upset, that I backed into a pole and caused a lot of damage to our van.

When I got home, I delivered this news. We spent the night crying and taking turns hugging Sibley. Poor Sibley! She didn't know what was going on. The dreadful morning came when we had to surrender her. None of us could eat. Our eyes were red and swollen from crying.

When we arrived at the drop-off point, the girls did not want to let her go into the school's van. The van was filled with cages, or crates. Rachel was the last to say goodbye to Sibley. When she gave her to the driver, she called her Cruella de Vil, a character from the movie, *101 Dalmatians*. I bet this was the first time the driver was called Cruella de Vil.

Giving up an adorable pup was a growing experience for all of us. We all learned that we have to take the good with the bad – the happy with the sad. We learned that doing a selfless act for others took away the sting of letting go. I also understood that each foster home/puppy raiser played an important role for the school. Guiding Eyes needed the time to weed out the pups that would not succeed as a guide dog, as well as the others who experienced "success." In the eyes of the school, we were all successful, and were treated as such. I also realized that if it was this hard to let a pup go after two years, what would it be like to let my daughters go when they moved out? Letting Sibley go was "bad news" in the eyes of the girls. The "good news" was that we received, Franklin, another guide dog pup, a day later. A week later, we also received the news that Sibley did not pass her tests and that she was coming back to us. So now, we had Franklin and Sibley. And the fun began.

Dear Father,
Thank you for creating dogs for this special purpose. It's amazing to think that certain dogs were meant to serve people with disabilities. We all are grateful for this learning experience. What we learned through our involvement in this program has remained with each one of us. Thank you for teaching us about unconditional love through having a dog. I often said that dog is God spelled backwards because you wanted to teach us what unconditional love was really like. Thank you for the love we received from Sibley, Franklin, and the rest of the dogs in our care.

About Discipline

Whenever my children misbehave and deliberately break a rule (especially one that I just reminded them of) it's hard to explain that I am disciplining them because I love them. Their response of, "yeah, sure," shows me that my message of love went right over their heads. There is a definite tie between love and discipline. It says in the Bible that the Lord disciplines those whom He loves. (Proverbs 3:11-12)

When I think about my daughters, I think about the intense love I have for them. I love them so much that I want them to be safe and protected. I love them even when they mess up, but I love them too much to let them act this way. Because I love them, I want them to achieve their life's goals. I wish them good health and self-esteem, but not pride. I want them to have joy in their lives. I pray that they have healthy relationships, especially in their adult years. I pray that they will grow up to be responsible adults, doing some line of work that uses their true gifts and makes them fulfilled. Most of all, I want them to have a personal relationship with God.

In order for these things to happen, I had to fulfill my role as a parent and discipline them when it was necessary. As hard as it was for me to confront, I needed to step in when they were doing something that would harm themselves or others. It's so much easier to let things slide, isn't it? Our rules were the guard rails that they needed.

As I think about the relationship between love and discipline, I realize that my Creator loves me so much, and the rest of the human race, that He gave us a set of rules to follow: the Ten Commandments. I grew up with so many images of God as a strict, angry disciplinarian, with oodles of rules and regulations.

As I have come to know my heavenly Father, I realize that this is so far from the truth. Our Father created us and knows what's best for us. The rules are really guardrails for life. As His kid, I have to respect His rules, authority, and wisdom. Too often, I have broken the rules and strayed off the path that I was on. It must have hurt the Father terribly when I broke His rules, because it damaged our relationship. I wonder if He cringes or cries when we commit sins?

Dear Father,
Help me, Your daughter, to feel Your love deeper than ever before, so that keeping Your commandments won't be a chore, but a joy. Help me to always accept Your loving discipline and help me to love and discipline my children well.

Christmas Preparations

This year, Advent really snuck up on me. It was the second week of December and I thought I would be ready for Christmas by now, but I had yet to unbury my Advent wreath. Oh well. Just another material trapping, right? Christmas will happen whether I am fully decorated or not. As I prepare for the celebration of Christmas, the birth of Jesus, I am doubly blessed to watch my girls anticipate the holiday.

For today, I am only going to focus on their HOPE. I asked them what they were hoping for? They replied that they were hoping that we would get to cut down our Christmas tree, instead of buying it from a lot. They hoped that we would get to bake all their favorite Christmas cookies. They hoped that Santa would get their wish list in time. Each day, they seemed to have another hope to add to the list.

What is my hope for Christmas this year? I hope to reach a delicate balance between the necessary Christmas preparations and time to pray, meditate, and spend quality time with my family. I hope for the promise of Christ which is PEACE that surpasses all understanding. I hope that this peace will be evermore deepened in my life and that more of my friends and family members will also experience amazing serenity. I hope to be more sensitive to the Lord's promptings. I hope that my eyes will not be plagued with tunnel vision, only looking straight ahead at what I have to do, but to look around and see those in need. And then I prayed for the energy to take care of my family.

Most of all, I hope for the second coming of Christ and all that His reign promises. At Christmas, we all catch a momentary glimpse of Heaven.

The love, the spirit of sharing and caring, is like heaven on earth. I eagerly hope for the time when Christ's peace, justice, love, and happiness will reign forever. And thanks to Christmas, we are reminded once again of this hope on Jesus' birthday.

Dear Father,
As my children hope for the coming of Christmas, help me to keep my spirit of hope alive of Your second coming. As we prepare for this important holiday, help me to be even more mindful that I need to be prepared to meet You one day. Help me to keep me to keep my eyes fixed on what's eternal, and not the material stuff that's passing away.

The Manger

Today, my kids and I unpacked our manger, which we had stored in our barn. Even though it was wrapped in plastic, dust still seemed to get into the manger. As we set it up, Rachel, who is always reluctant to throw anything away, made an exception here. To spruce up the manager before placing the statues of the Holy Family, she decided to throw away all the old straw. She carefully dusted the manger and placed clean straw inside.

When I thought about this Advent exercise of cleaning the manger, I was struck with the similarity between that manger and our lives. Each Advent, I try to get rid of "old stuff" to make room for the new. I sort through toys and books with the girls to fill up a donation box and make room for the gifts they are about to receive. Even though they know they are going to receive presents on Christmas, they are sometimes reluctant to give up a favorite sweater, or toy, or book. They like to hang on to things, just like I do. Why is this? Why do we carry that attachment spirit with us?

I also thought about cleaning out the manger of my heart, which is the spiritual purpose of Advent. We need to prepare our hearts for the coming of Christ. Whether He comes on a cloud in His second coming, or we meet Him after we die, we still must be prepared. What a great time to identify and purge the sin in our lives to make way for a closer relationship to Jesus. What a wonderful time to ask for the grace to change a bad habit, heal a resentful heart, or forgive a broken relationship. I taught my girls that anything against God is sin. We need to get rid of it so we can have a relationship with God. One Advent, when they were older, we wrote down our prayers, our thoughts, and our good deeds on a slip of straw colored paper and placed them in the manger in lieu of straw. By the end of the month, we had a pile of "straw" to welcome Baby Jesus.

Dear Father,
Thank you for this reminder that we should not be holding onto things, only holding onto You. Help us get rid of our sin and excess baggage, which keeps us from drawing near to You. Help us turn our eyes away from the material gifts and focus on all the spiritual gifts that You continuously give us. Show us how to use these spiritual gifts to help others and build the Kingdom.

After You have cleansed me, fill the empty spaces within my heart with new behaviors, attitudes, and virtues. Give me the grace to not only focus on the present moment, but the eternal. Help me to remember that our time here on earth is quickly passing away and help those reading this to pass these truths on to their children and grandchildren.

We Plan but Sometimes God Has Other Plans

"Life is what happens while you are making other plans." Ever heard this phrase? Each year, we sit down as a family and plan what the month of December will look like. What special thing do we want to do in Advent as a family? What do we have to do to prepare for Christmas? What activities/parties are planned for school, Sunday school, and clubs? When you have a family, planning is key to getting anything done, at least in my case.

This particular year, Thanksgiving came late, which meant less time to prepare for Christmas. Even though I had simplified Christmas in years past, I still felt the need to do charitable works in the community and make a magical Christmas for my girls. Then a super flu bug attacked the kids and then me, keeping me in bed for three weeks. I thought, "How on earth am I supposed to get ready for Christmas?" As the days ticked by, all I could do was lie in bed and pray. I was even too sick to read or watch TV. This scenario was actually a blessing in disguise. While I was down, I realized that all I really needed to do to get ready for Christmas was to pray and prepare my heart.

When I realized this, I was able to pass this peace onto my girls. I reviewed our "to do" list and crossed out many unnecessary items. I gave up writing Christmas cards and the infamous Christmas letter. I stopped sending Christmas packages and even gave up my Christmas baking (this was a hard one for me). We cut way down on Christmas decorations and decorated the tree later than ever before. I joked with the girls that if we waited until Christmas Eve to get a tree, they just may give it to us for free. Miraculously, the wrapping got done and even the house was cleaned before Christmas.

This year, I realized that the most important thing about Christmas was finding Jesus. By prayer and centering on the Lord, I had more peace. I cared more about spending quality time with my family, being well enough to go to church on Christmas Eve (one tradition I will never surrender) and having joy in my heart.

Dear Father,
Thank you for being patient with me during this Advent and reminding me what is truly important. Do you shake your head when You see humans running around making Christmas preparations? Are You sad when you see how commercial this holiday has become? Are You appalled that most people celebrate the birthday of Jesus, yet don't know Him or believe in Him at all? I am so thankful that despite of our inadequacies, You are patient and kind with us, and Your love is eternal.

Parenting Isn't for Cowards

Years ago, I read a book by Dr. James Dobson called "*Parenting Isn't for Cowards*." Boy, isn't that the truth? Parenting is hard! Nothing in the world prepared me to become a mom. Even though I had countless hours of babysitting under my belt, it wasn't the same. As the second oldest of six kids, I baby sat my younger brothers. George and Tony were babies when I was in upper elementary and middle school. Even with all this experience, it didn't prepare me for the joys and rigors of parenting.

Sadly, we often parent the way we were parented. Some of it good --- some of it not so good. When we adopted Rachel, she was only 11 weeks old. Her foster mother sent her "schedule" with her. I thought, "Gee, we are all set. This is going to be a piece of cake. All I have to do is follow the schedule!" Unfortunately, I learned rather quickly that 11-week old babies can't read schedules. There certainly was no manual to show me how to take care of this infant, let alone parent her to adulthood.

I used to wonder, how could I parent when there is no manual? Fortunately, Lord, You have given us one: the Bible. The challenge for me, as a new mother, was finding the time to read it. My prayer life certainly changed drastically after Rachel joined our family. Looking back, I can see the value of Bible-based teaching in child rearing. If I had a "do over," I would spend more time contacting the "Throne" and less time talking on the phone.

Dear Father,

You have taken care of showing us how to parent when you gave us Your Living Word. I pray that more young people, that we mentor, will use it as their main parenting tool. I pray that my children, who have children of their own, will pick it up and use it as the valuable "owner's manual" for their babies. Please put the desire in my heart to spend more time in Your Word. As we get older, we still need your wisdom as answers to problems. Luckily, the answers are in your Word. Give me the grace to obey.

Daddy Is Our Comfort and Strength

On the way home from work at a boarding school for emotionally disturbed clients, my sister fell asleep behind the wheel after working a double shift. It was a two-lane road in the Berkshire Mountains in Massachusetts. We learned that she hit another car head on when she crossed the double yellow line. We were thankful that the other driver was not seriously hurt. My sister, however, had multiple lacerations on her face, a concussion and whiplash, a broken arm, and a shattered ankle. She was a mess. We were thankful she was still alive.

The night after we visited my sister in ICU, I thought about the reaction of my daughters at seeing their aunt. Rachel, our five-year-old, just looked at her in awe. On the way out of ICU, Rachel's eyes started to tear up, and she was terribly sad and shaken.

Stephanie's response was altogether different. As a two-year-old, she had her feelings right on the surface. She was brutally honest and held nothing back. She looked at her Aunt Mary for a second and buried her face in her father's shoulder. Her entire body was tense. But the longer her father held her, the more relaxed she became.

Looking at my daughters' reaction to tragedy teaches the way I need to be with the Father. First, I must feel my feelings like Rachel did. I have to let everything out and allow my feelings to surface. I have to acknowledge the shock, the grief, the fear, and the pain of the moment. Then, just as Stephanie did, I must go to the Father for comfort. I only need to nuzzle against His big shoulders and let my tears flow. The Father is my faithful, 24-hour source of comfort, love, and guidance.

Dear Father,

Help me to trust in your fatherly love for me. Help me to run to You for comfort before I reach out to anyone else. Help me to reach for the heavenly Throne instead of the phone. Help me to remember that You are always there for me. Help me to detach from earthly sources of consolation and pleasure and worldly things, which never satisfy me.

Filled With the Spirit

When Rachel was only three, I took her to a Charismatic Mass at our church. We liked it so much that we attended that Mass frequently while Daddy and baby Stephanie stayed home. From a very early age, Rachel heard me and other believers praying in tongues. This is a gift of the Holy Spirit, where people pray in a "prayer language" only known to the Holy Spirit. For some it may be "weird." But to Rachel and our family, this was normal.

Many times, after Mass, I would go up for prayer, where people do the "laying on of hands." They prayed for healing or other special things like provision, grace, patience, a family member etc. Many times, I was overwhelmed by the presence of the Holy Spirit and fell to the ground. This was called "slain in the spirit" and was a common occurrence in our church. Rachel would often sit by me on the floor until I woke up from my "God dream," as she called them.

Rachel was very open to the working of the Holy Spirit and never once questioned or judged the practices of the Charismatic believers as weird or odd. She was a strong believer and accepted this as the way to pray and worship. Her younger sister, Stephanie, followed in her footsteps when she was the same age.

One morning, Rachel was really sick when she woke up for Pre-kindergarten. She came to me and said that she better not go to school that day because she didn't want to give her "bad throat germs" to the other students. (I wondered why adults weren't half as smart?) I sent her back to bed and brought in some Tylenol for her high fever and a cold washcloth for her head. I asked if she wanted anything else and she said, “Yes, Mommy. Could you please pray over me in Tongues and in English?” I was floored! When she was sick, the first thing she thought of was to stay home and pray. She said that she “wanted Daddy God to make her better – so you better ask in BOTH languages.”

How often I try everything else FIRST and when nothing else is working, then I go to the Lord and pray. God must just shake His head and wonder why I didn't ask Him FIRST, like my little daughter. I wonder if He ever gets frustrated with me.

Dear Father,
You always promised that whatever we ask for in Your Son's name, and believe we will receive, You will give it to us. Help me to be more mindful that I should always approach You FIRST, just like Rachel did.

I'm Just a Bobbing Cork in the Sea of Life

One weekend, I needed some "mommy time out." I was getting burned out being a wife and mother and working in ministry, so my hubby sent me away to Florida for a long weekend while he took care of the girls.

On my first morning in Ft. Lauderdale, it was warm and sunny. There wasn't a cloud in the sky, but it was windy. The biggest gift was being able to go snorkeling off the coral reef. As I dove from the boat into the ocean, I truly felt the Father's power and majesty. It was a choppy day to be snorkeling, for sure. The winds were kicking up 15 mph with higher gusts. The waves were cresting between five and ten feet. Why the boat company took us out, I will never know. I really felt so small and helpless. It seemed like I was a small cork, bobbing in the ferocious sea. The waves tossed our boat around as if it were a piece of driftwood.

I really felt like a little child out there today, I recalled the initial fear I had as the waves got even higher. As I jumped into the ocean, I remembered that You were only a prayer away. In a split second, as I prayed for You to protect me, I became peaceful and relaxed. I could finally enjoy this whole experience.

Dear Father,

I thank you that when Your child cries out to You, You do not delay in revealing your peaceful presence. Stay with me always, Father. Just like the ocean, Earth can also be a scary place.

God vs. Money

Today I walked around the marina in Ft. Lauderdale. It was so beautiful. Sparkling blue water contrasted with pristine white yachts and boats. This moment reminded me of the time our family went to see our friend's new home that they just custom built. These yachts, mansions, and our friend's home were opulent and more that we could ever afford.

By contrast, we were living in a "starter home," which was a modest raised ranch in a middle class neighborhood outside of Albany. We never planned to stay there for more than a few years, but it became our permanent home. We had a lot of medical expenses for infertility treatment and adoption expenses. After we adopted Rachel, I sold my successful public relations company to be a stay-at-home mom and live on one income. Things were tight, living paycheck to paycheck, but we were happy and content.

After riding home from our friend's mansion with our daughters, we pulled into our driveway and Rachel said, "It's so good to be home! I just love this house. I never want to move." God and money. The two are incompatible. It says in Scripture that we cannot serve two masters, God and money. And I'm beginning to understand that.

There is freedom in not owning very much. We know many well-off families. I find that the more they own, the more they want. The more they have, the more they have to take care of and worry about. The less you have, the more freedom you have to spend time with your children, your friends, in prayer, and in ministry. There's an inner joy in hungering for spiritual gifts and heavenly wealth and beginning to attain them in this life. Rachel was so correct. I love our simple home and unassuming lifestyle. Home is where you are loved and free to express your feelings. You always said, "Seek first the Kingdom of God and everything else will be given to you." (Matthew 6:33 NIV). I stand on this promise.

Dear Father,

Thank you for the gift of Your Son, who through His word and example shows us the way to Kingdom living. Thank you for the inner peace and joy that comes from fellowship with You, and for the wisdom of the Holy Spirit, which keeps us yearning for heavenly treasures. Thanks for reminding me that if I live only for myself, one day, at the end of my life, all I will have is myself. But if I live for You, I will have You now and the riches of Heaven forever.

Separation

I have been away from my family for two and one half days. Although I needed some respite, not a moment went by that I did not think about my family. Though geography may separate us, no one can separate me from the love of my family. I am and always will be Rachel and Stephanie's mother. That longing to see them will always be there.

At times, Lord, I feel that geography separates us. I have never seen You face to face. I have no idea what Heaven looks like. The more I get to know You, the more homesick I get for Heaven. Your promises, that are spelled out in Scripture, are true. I know that no one can separate us from the love of God through Christ Jesus. I know that in Your house are many mansions and that You are preparing a place for me, as I write this. The longing to see You face to face is real.

Dear Daddy God,
Thank you, Father, for never letting a second go by that You don't think of me and all You have created. If You stopped thinking of us, we would cease to be. Father, help me to turn my thoughts towards You, as Your thoughts are always with me.

Unique

Today, at the aquarium, I must have seen 100 different species of fish. They varied in size, shape, color and patterns. The girls marveled at how unique each fish was. Yes, some may be part of the same genus or species, but each one is so different.

It is the same with the human race. Rachel and Stephanie are both being raised by the same parents, but each girl is a wondrous miracle of creation. You formed us to be totally unique and breathed an eternal soul into us at the moment we were conceived.

I marvel that each of our fingerprints and our DNA is unduplicated in the entire universe. How can anyone doubt Your existence? Even each snowflake has a different pattern. And we know how much snow we got last winter!

Dear Father,

You are the Author of all life. How could anyone doubt Your existence, but so many do! I praise You because we are fearfully and wonderfully made. How wonderful are Your works. I praise You that you took care of every detail in creation. Nothing went unnoticed. Father, thank you for Your great love for me and for taking care of every detail of my world. I am in wonder that in spite of all You are doing to create and maintain the universe, You still desire to be in constant communion with me and with each one of us. I praise You now and forever, Lord!

Choose Life

Here we are again. January 22, the anniversary of Roe vs Wade. As I picketed today with our two adopted daughters, I reflected on an incident that took place right in front of Planned Parenthood, three years ago.

Rachel was three at that time. We were walking and praying in front of this abortion clinic and Rachel was carrying a sign that read, "Adoption Not Abortion." The media were there, and they were playing their usual game of "Stump the Pro-lifers" with their questions.

The ABC reporter decided to interview Rachel to see if she knew why she was there, or was her mom merely using her as a prop. He leaned down with his microphone and asked, "Do you know why you are here little girl?" "Uh huh," she replied. "Why?" he continued. "To protest," she innocently answered. The reporter looked shocked! "To protest what?" he questioned. "The killing of babies," Rachel replied. "They are killing babies in there," as she pointed to the building, "and that's not right, is it?" This male reporter, with tears in his eyes, turned to his cameraman and yelled, "Cut!"

Unfortunately, this interview never made it on TV. Abortion IS killing a baby, but that's too messy and true for them to report. It's easier to make it a political issue or an issue about choice. It's much less offensive that way.

I was so proud of Rachel that day. With her childlike innocence, she was able to speak the truth to that reporter. Her witness was also heard by the cameraman and the people surrounding us. The funny thing was, I never told Rachel that abortion was wrong. As we drove to the event, I merely defined it. At three years old, she was able to process a definition with her own moral judgement and convey that to the media. If only the whole world could see what abortion is through the eyes of a little one! We would be so much better off. Babies would have a chance at life and the moms would not be emotionally scarred for life because of this traumatic experience.

Dear Father,
I can't think of a day that hurts your heart more! When I look back on the number of babies killed since 1973, it breaks my heart, especially when there are so many persons waiting to adopt. But You are the Almighty Creator of each little one. How horrible it must be for You to watch what is going on. How awful that precious unborn babies are killed on the altar of political correctness and "choice." Each baby is one of Your most precious creations. I praise and thank you that these babies are with You in Heaven. Father, I pray that anyone reading this story will have a heart that truly feels what you feel. Please forgive our nation, Father, for what we have done in the name of "choice."

Fear Is My Worst Enemy

As I compare my life to the lives of my young children, I am struck with a major difference: the amount of fear that I carry. So many of my fears are tied to my past. One of my fears has always been running out of money. I grew up in a middle class family where my dad worked two jobs to provide for Mom, six kids, and my grandma. When he passed away suddenly, I was only a freshman in college. Now with the only breadwinner in the family gone, my mom, who had spent her whole life as a stay-at-home mom, was forced to work. Money was extremely tight and the benefits we received were not enough to pay our bills. We received food stamps for a while. My mom was too proud or embarrassed to shop in our usual grocery store, so she would drive to another neighborhood.

As I was raising my children, I feared that I would die before they were grown. I imagined how hard their lives would be without me. I breathed a sigh of relief when I passed 44, the age of my dad when he died. I rejoiced when I saw them graduate from high school and then college.

As I think about Rachel and Stephanie's lack of fear, compared to mine, could it be that they felt safe and secure? Or maybe they just haven't lived long enough to accumulate unnecessary baggage. I believe that if children learn to trust at an early age, and their needs are met, they will have less fear. Kids also live in the present more than adults and aren't obsessed with past memories. They also don't worry about the future as much as adults.

When I look at my laundry list of fears, I am amazed at how future-oriented they are, yet also rooted in the past. Worry is fear that hasn't said its prayers. To live in freedom, I need to sort through my fears and let them go, one at a time. I need to imitate my children by living in the present moment. I have discovered that the "One Day at a Time" philosophy, from the 12-step program (a program that helps people recover from their addictions), is better practiced by children than adults.

Dear Father,
It says in your Word that "There is no fear in love. But perfect love drives out fear, because fear has to do with punishment. The one who fears is not made perfect in love." (1 John 4:18) Gently remove my fears and replace them with a deep, deep trust in You. Help me to live more in the present, like my little girls. Help me to let go of the painful memories of the past and the harmful thoughts of the future. You alone are perfect Love. Draw me close to Your heart.

Little Imitators

The other night while I was out with friends, Rachel, our five-year old, told my husband that she was watching me all the time to see "how to be all grown up." While I always knew that children, especially during the formative years, were great imitators, the comment really hit me. I realized that my girls would be imitating more than the physical aspects of being a woman, such as hygiene, fashion, applying makeup, and doing their hair. They would also be learning how to cook and bake, clean house, do outdoor work, take care of a car, and the ins and outs of bargain shopping. While these things are important, there is something way more important.

When they look at my emotional state, what will they find to imitate? What will they be imitating when handling stress, resolving conflicts in relationships, forgiveness, and dealing with anger? How will they identify their feelings and express themselves appropriately? What will they be imitating when prioritizing and finishing tasks? How will the girls be learning to cope with their fears, their faults, and the shortcomings of others?

As if all these things were not overwhelming enough, I also thought about the spiritual side of life. So many parents focus only on the physical and emotional aspects of their children. They forget that their children also have a soul and need spiritual food to grow.

What will the girls be imitating from me in their prayer life, in faith-building experiences, or in performing works of charity? What spiritual values would they learn from me? As they form their value system, will they be based in faith hope and love? There is so much to teach them and so little time!

Dear Father,
I realize that parenting is an overwhelming job and a tremendous responsibility. Without You, Father, I wouldn't know where to start. With Your help, I am learning to trust in Your wisdom, goodness, and providence, especially in the "hard to parent" areas. I am learning that I am not perfect, and I am going to make mistakes. In fact, who hasn't blown it now and then? I realize that You are the only perfect parent and that You are eager to give me all I need to parent and mold the lives of these two daughters you have loaned me for a while. As long as I keep trying and asking for Your grace, I'm pleasing You, my Daddy God.

I am also learning (and this is the hardest lesson to practice daily) to imitate You, just as my children imitate me. I need to constantly look to You as the role model for my parenting. When I try to parent on my own power, I fall flat on my face each time. I need to look to You, especially when I am super stressed and don't know how to handle a situation. I need to imitate Your parenting style. At times, I also think about the qualities of Mary, Your mom. She had to go through so many difficult trials, yet Scripture reveals that "she pondered things up in her heart." Her motherhood is such an inspiration to me.

Thank you for giving me the strength and wisdom to be a parent and believe that there is no such thing as a perfect parent, except for You. Help me always to imitate You.

THE MIDDLE YEARS

LETTERS FROM 15 YEARS AGO
Middle and high school years

Each season of life has its challenges. There is a saying: "Little children, little problems. Bigger children.... Bigger problems." As if raising adolescents was not hard enough, these were the years when my first marriage ended. Rachel was 13 and Stephanie was only 10. I found myself in desperate times. It was during these years that I leaned on my friends and my faith. Sadly, my mom and siblings were not "there" for me. Through many days and nights of praying, I came to realize that God would never leave me or forsake me. He became my best friend, my rock, the anchor of my soul, my provider, counselor, and husband.

My Daddy

Today is the anniversary of my dad's death. November 1, 1973, was a defining moment. His sudden death made my mom a widow at age 40. Dad was only 44 and I was 17 and a freshman in college. As I think about that date, I remember how scared I was that we weren't going to make it. My dad was the rock of our family and now he was gone. None of us were prepared for this news nor ready to live without him. I try to think of this time to put myself in my daughters' shoes as they try to deal with our divorce. A somewhat happy family, intact, and functional in their eyes, was now torn apart. The stability they knew was over. Their stay-at-home mom now had to go back to work. They didn't get to see their dad every day. They were the only kids going through this in our circle of friends, neighbors, or family.

Dear Father,

I am amazed by the inner courage and strength You gave all of us at the time my dad died. Each of us children played a special part in honoring his life. When I think about how present You were to me during those awful days of hearing the news, shopping for flowers and a coffin, and going through four days of a wake, I just want to cry. Just as You provided for us kids, You also provided for my girls. We always had food, shelter, clothes, medicine, and even the extras like music lessons, braces, and a vacation. All of Your provision was so "behind the scenes" to my girls, but it was clearly there to me. Thank you for loving Your children so much and being our rock in the most devasting time in our lives. Help me to always lean on You and trust that You are working things out behind the scenes, 24 hours a day, even if I don't feel Your presence. You are an amazing Father.

Why Don't You Listen?

Today was one of those days where I had a mile-long "to do list." Out-of-town company was coming. I was planning a birthday party for my daughter. I was barking out orders like a drill sarge. I had a deadline and so much to do. Trying to get my teenagers to clean their room and help with housework was at the top of the list. Sound familiar?

In desperation on this chaotic day, I yelled, "If only you girls would keep quiet, you would listen to what I have to say!" This must be the same thing our heavenly parent says to us. When the Lord wants to speak to me and I am doing a headless chicken routine, shouting at my kids, I am certainly not in "listening to God" mode. Then I thought of my prayer time. How much time do I spend talking instead of listening? Does God wish I would just shut up and listen to Him? I'm certain that if I started my day by listening to Him, things would go much smoother.

I've learned that children love the sound of a parent's voice, whether in conversation or reading a story. They prefer gentle questions over brusque commands. I love our conversations with my girls when I give them time to talk. Just like our kids love when we listen to them, I love when my Father listens to me. Even more, He loves when I listen to Him.

Dear Father,
Help me to know when to shut my mouth and hear Your gentle, loving voice speaking to me. Cultivate my prayer time so that I do more listening and less talking. Help me to be a better listener in all my relationships.

The Runaway Teenager

One of the house rules I had for my teenagers was always let me know where they were going and give me the phone number of the friend's house. This was well over 30 years ago before the pager, cell phone, and phone app that locates your child. Kidnapping was on the rise since the time when I was a kid (the dinosaur age, my girls will tell you). Having a missing child was one of my worst fears. That is why I had very strict rules, or boundaries, and appropriate consequences for crossing the boundary.

One Thanksgiving after dinner, my daughter told us that she was going down to her best friend's house. This house was in walking distance, in a very safe neighborhood, and I knew the parents well. This family helped raise my oldest daughter and I helped to raise theirs. Imagine the shock when I called down to them to send my daughter home, and she wasn't there! In fact, she was never there. It was already 10 or 11 o'clock and I could not even imagine where she could be, or with whom. This family enlisted the help of the neighbors to call around and look outside for my daughter.

I immediately called the police and filed a missing person's report. I was trying to keep from crying, but it was hard. She was only 13 years old at the time. All the negative possibilities ran through my mind and I was sick to my stomach. One hour passed, and then another hour, and another. Finally, around 1:00 a.m., the police department placed an officer at our home in case she made it home. The rest were frantically looking for her. The kind police officer stayed with us and kept us informed as the search went on.

Somewhere between 3 and 4 a.m., Rachel came strolling through the door. She was safe and she was home. I was so thankful to see her but so angry at the same time. The police peppered her with questions. "Where have you been? With whom?" We learned that she left in a car with an older teen that she met online. Oh, my Lord, how dangerous was this? She made it all the way to a mall that was 10 miles away.

After the police's inquisition, she had to deal with mine. "Why did you break the cardinal rule of the house? How did you get home? What were you doing all this time?" These were only some of my questions.

By the time we got to bed, the sun was about to rise. She had never done something this outrageous, and so I had to think of an appropriate consequence. While I was so happy that she was safe at home, my blood was boiling at the complete disregard for us and herself. Her disobedience could have turned out very differently.

In our conversation about boundaries and crossing the line, I also thought of the boundaries that God sets up for us. He is a loving parent; in fact, He is the perfect parent. He disciplines those He loves, which is everyone. He makes rules for us to follow to protect us, not to punish. Just like we have rules for our children's benefit, He has rules for us.

As I thought about this, I also reflected on the verse in the Bible, "the wages of sin is death. But the free gift of God is eternal life in Christ Jesus." I thought that wages of her sin of running away could have easily been death. There were too many stories of young girls running away that were never found, or found dead, miles from their home. I was so thankful that our Father was merciful and kind and allowed our daughter to come home. So many parents don't have this same outcome.

Dear Father,

I am grateful that You brought my daughter home. Thank you for taking care of each of us, all the time. As a mom, I want to keep my girls close to my side, but that isn't always possible. I am thankful, my loving Father, that You never take Your eyes off Your children.

Thank you for showing me Your heart and how it feels when just one of Your kids runs away from home. You have given each of us free will, which will always be a mystery to me. How hard it must be for You when we use our free will to engage in destructive behavior. How sad it is for You when even one of us runs away. But how happy and relieved You must be when we find our way back to you.

Thank you for loving me so completely that You gave me a set of guidelines, or rules, to follow and keep me safe. And when I have broken Your commandments, thank you for loving me so much that You take me back. Now I understand what it means to "love the sinner and hate the sin."

Too Loving?

When Rachel was in middle school, she went on a church retreat. The retreat center was over an hour from our house in the Adirondack mountains. It was located in a beautiful but remote setting. We had to travel mostly on a two-lane road to get there. One of the biggest rules on the retreat was keeping the sexes separated. No boys were allowed on the girls' floor and visa versa. Imagine the shock when I got a call, sometime after dark, to come and pick up my daughter. Rachel allowed one of the boys to use the shower in their suite, since all the boys' showers had long lines. She was sitting on the floor outside her suite to prevent any girls from entering. While this seemed pretty safe, it still was a major infraction. Her motive was good, but her action was very wrong.

I was not a happy camper, since I had to work the next day and this drama was way past my bedtime. I had to drive over an hour, on a winding dark road, avoiding deer, to pick her up. All the way home, we talked about obedience. While I never wanted to squelch her loving and kind nature, she still had to understand and respect authority.

The church retreat incident reminded me of when Rachel was in Kindergarten. The first week of school, her teacher called me at home. "Oh no," I thought. "What could possibly be wrong?" She called to say that Rachel was "too loving." Um ….. that was a first! How could someone, especially a 5-year old, be too loving? She went on to say that each morning, she would say hello by hugging everyone, including the teacher. Before dismissal, Rachel would hug everyone goodbye. This was the way that our family and our church operated. We were, and still are, big huggers. It was hard to explain to an affectionate child, that she can't be that way at school, because it may make some children "uncomfortable."

It was difficult to reprimand her in both situations when her motive was love. This was one of the many times I had to pray for wisdom to find the appropriate consequence.

Dear Father,
You see all our actions, but You also see our motives. Help us to practice loving kindness in all situations, but practice respect for authority overall. Help us to be obedient to the rules set before us. Give me wisdom as I parent my kids. Your answers to these situations supersede anything I could ever think of.

No End to Generosity

Before I had children, I took my parents for granted. I didn't acknowledge all they did for us and the sacrifices they made. I also never realized how expensive it was to raise one child. Some sources put that number at $250,000 per child! We are trying to do it for less, but without keeping close records, we have no idea how much we spent.

At every age, we desired and tried to give our girls everything imaginable. We sacrificed buying things for ourselves so that we could afford to buy what they needed. As they went off to school, the bills increased. We had school supplies, music lessons, dance lessons, braces, and lots of shoes! They were growing fast and always needed shoes and clothes. When they became teenagers, they wanted name-brand jeans and sneakers. We saved and sacrificed, and we bought them what they needed.

Their material needs were only one part of the equation. The other side of parenting was sacrificing time. I don't do well unless I have eight hours of sleep. When they were newborns, I didn't get much sleep. As they started sleeping through the night, it was so much easier. Bath, bottle, and bedtime. Now I could have a few moments to myself.

Then the sleepovers in our home started. As tired as I was, I stayed up until the last girl fell asleep. Several years later, they would have sleepovers upstairs in our barn. It was a short walk between our house and barn, but at 3:00 a.m., when I went to check on them, it seemed like miles. And who can forget "Midnight Bowling?" What moron invented this? Don't they know that parents need their sleep? I dreaded the night

I drew the short straw and had to collect the girls, their friends, and drive them home in our mini-van. How did I ever live through this season? Here's a news flash for parents of babies: the sleep deprivation thing goes on until kids move out.

Being emotionally present was equally challenging. There were nights when they wanted to talk, or vent about something that happened that day. We stayed up until the wee hours to talk, even though they had school and I had work the next day. Some days I was so tired of being the "on call" single parent. I didn't think I would live through this. It was so exhausting.

Dear Father,
Unlike us frail humans, You are there for each one of us 24 hours a day, seven days a week. Thank you that You never get tired of talking with us and that Your resources to provide for our every need never runs out. Thank you, Father, for giving me the strength and grace to navigate through those first 18 years of Rachel and Stephanie's lives. Thank you for the stamina of being a single parent. But as You well know, we never stop being a parent. Well into their 20s and 30s, their needs continue. I am grateful for the wisdom to parent our kids as they get older. Help me to always turn to You for parental advice.

No Condemnation

The night after Rachel ran away, my husband decided to move out. He packed his things and drove to a friend's house. This was the first official day of our separation. The feeling in the air was so heavy. While I hated to see him go, I was relieved with the peace that filled the house once he was gone.

I can't describe the feelings I had as I watched him move his belongings towards the car. This moment had been coming for a long time. I had lived with many stressful days for over two years. But actually, coming to this point was gut wrenching, mainly for the girls. At 10 and 13 years old, it is hard to lose a dad. While he was still physically present to them, he wasn't the same emotionally. I cried as I watched them say goodbye to their dad, not knowing when they would see him again. We did not know at the time if this was a temporary separation, or something permanent. I saw the fear in their eyes, along with the sorrow.

Later that day, I walked into Rachel's room and she was crying. "If only I had been a better daughter, this never would have happened. If only I listened more, maybe things would be different. If only I had not run away last night, he would have stayed." I said, "Stop right there! You are blaming yourself for something that had nothing to do with you." She had a hard time believing me. I can't remember how long she condemned herself for her dad's problems and his moving out, but it was a while.

Isn't that the way we are with the Father? Don't we have a hard time forgiving ourselves and a harder time accepting that some things just are not our fault? As her mom, I tried everything to convince her not to take on her dad's blame and shame. Looking back, time and prayer were the only things that worked.

Dear Father,

It says in your Word that "There is no condemnation in those who are in Christ Jesus". I'm also reminded of the story where the woman in the Bible was about to be stoned. How gentle and forgiving You were towards her. In Your life, you cast out condemnation and replaced it with Your divine mercy. Thank you for giving me the grace to show that to Rachel. Thank you for working in her heart to realize that she is not a condemned kid, but a cherished daughter of Yours and mine.

Parenting Isn't for Cowards

Someone gave me a book on parenting by Dr. James Dobson from Focus on the Family Ministries. While kids don't come with an owner's manual, there are many great resources to navigate the treacherous waters of parenting. Each phase has its own challenges. What may have worked when they were babies doesn't transfer over to toddlers, elementary school and so on. I loved the title of this book. It takes a lot of courage to be responsible for another life, let alone three lives, for 18 plus years. Cowards do not stand a chance in the parenting arena. So much of parenting is trial and error. It takes extraordinary courage to function with a house full of teens.

There is nothing in all the books that prepare you for the pre-teen or teen years. Adolescence — the phase that some parents confess made them question why they ever wanted kids in the first place. I was no different. I remember the days when each of the kids turned from loving, pleasant, kind, and obedient to moody, disobedient, unpleasant monsters.

I longed for the times when they were still in elementary school and they wanted to talk to me about their school day. I missed the cuddle time on the couch either reading a book or watching a movie together. I vaguely remember the instances when they would come to me for advice or help. Remember the days when you went to their elementary school to help in the classroom and they were so proud to have you there? I think I do.

Fast forward to adolescence:

> "How was school today?" "Fine."
>
> "Anything new today?" "Nope."
>
> "What's your favorite subject?" "Lunch"
>
> "Do you need help with that homework?" Grunt.
>
> "Why are you upset?" "You're too dumb to understand."
>
> "Want to go to the mall with me?" "Only if you let me bring a friend and walk a half a mile behind us."
>
> "I saw you at the concert." "Yes, and I thought I'd die of embarrassment when you came up afterwards and hugged me."

How on earth did I ever survive those days? I remember calling a friend and confiding that I love my kids, but I really don't like them right now. I often wonder if God feels the same way about us when we pull away. When we shut Him out and we think we can figure things out on our own, how does He react? While pulling away from parents is all part of the adolescence and teenage years, I don't think that God ever intended for us to pull away from Him.

I wonder why He doesn't stop us. He certainly could if He wanted. He gave us a free will and plenty of space for us to use it. I'm convinced that He loves us too much to interfere, because it's in those times that we learn and grow. When we make mistakes and realize that we weren't as smart as we thought, those are often the times when we come crawling back to God and admit our need for His wisdom and guidance.

Dear Father,

You are so patient with us. You watch as we pull away from You and learn the hard way. And still, You always take us back. I wish I could always be like that with our children. All three have different personalities and needs for independence. Lord, I can accept that they may not need us in the way that they did when they were growing up, but I pray that they realize their need for You.

Our Provider

Throughout all my years of going to church, I always heard that "God provides." I know that He has provided me with grace, wisdom, courage and comfort. But what about physical blessings, like money? How on earth does He do this?

When my dad died suddenly, and my mom (age 40) was left with six kids (ages 8 to 19) to raise, I have to admit that I was scared about how we were going to survive. I have come to realize that when my mom found work, that was a God thing since she was a stay-at-home mom for her whole married life. When friends or family sent a check with a note to Mom to encourage her, that was God. When my scholarships increased for the last three years of college, that was God providing for me.

When I was going through my divorce and became a single mom, I admit that I was fearful. I had sold my Public Relations firm 10 years prior to be a stay-at-home mom. This action alone reduced our family's income by 50%. Then when my ex wasn't working and not always paying child support, it was my responsibility to provide for the girls and me.

Yes, it was scary going back to the workforce after being home for so many years. I felt like my skills were rusty and I had very little self-confidence. One job I had applied for was about to be filled, when my resume came across the president's desk. She immediately called me and flew from Washington D.C. to Albany, New York, to conduct an interview. And then I was hired! Was that luck, as some would call it, or a divine appointment?

While I worked as the New York State Director for Families Against Mandatory Minimums, I was able to work out of a home office. This blessing allowed me to get my kids on and off the bus each day and still do my job, without lost time in commuting. After I put them to bed, I could go into my office and continue working. I also met so many wonderful people through this job, who supported me and loved me and the girls through this difficult time.

I was not making a lot of money at this job, but I was grateful. Little did I know that the income I was making was below the federal poverty line. But still, I paid the mortgage, the car payment, utilities, and bought food, all without ever going on public assistance. My girls were clothed, attended music and gymnastic lessons, and even took vacations every year. When they were in sports or cheerleading, I was able to buy their gear. Both girls had braces and Rachel even went to a private Catholic High School. I tithed at church and I believe the Lord took care of the rest of my needs.

One night, Stephanie spiked a fever. I had no Tylenol in the house, so I went to the store in the middle of a bad snowstorm. Nobody was out since it was so nasty. I was living paycheck to paycheck then and I was holding my breath until payday. I took my credit card because I had zero dollars in my wallet and checkbook. I was the only car in the parking lot, except for a few on the far end, which were probably store employees. As I walked into the store, I looked down in the snow and there was a $20 bill! Who did it belong to? There was nobody around, so I guess it was mine. I picked it up and thanked God for this unexpected blessing.

After I got home, I got on my knees and thanked God for taking care of me and the girls.

There was another week that I will never forget. On a Monday, I learned that our dog, who had been in remission from Lymphoma, had gotten sick again. The cancer was back, only this time, I could not afford the cancer treatments. On Tuesday, I found a lump on my breast, and I immediately thought “breast cancer.” On Wednesday, I went to the doctor for another problem and was told that I needed a total hysterectomy. On Thursday, I fell on the ice in the parking lot of Rachel’s school and got a concussion. And on Friday, I got a call from Washington that I was about to lose my job because funding was cut for the New York project.

Cancer, death, biopsy, surgery, concussion, and job loss – all in one week! Could things get any worse? I hated to ask. I would like to say that I was brave and trusting God, but I really lost it. I wondered how on earth I could go through a major surgery without a spouse or family to help me and the girls. I couldn’t imagine job hunting while I was home recuperating from surgery and couldn’t even drive to an interview. I wondered if my breast biopsy would be positive, and then I would have to face more surgery and treatment. I dreaded the day when I had to say goodbye to our beloved Labrador Retriever. My life had become so unraveled that my church friends called me “Mrs. Job.” Another neighbor kidded about never having to watch the soap operas. All she had to do was call me “to see what was new.”

While these trials were mounting and I didn't know how I would get through them, God did. He had a divine plan all lined up, but I couldn't see into the future. My adopted mom, Sr. Mary Clare, and my daughter, Rachel, accompanied me to the hospital the morning of my surgery. My boyfriend, Rick Tuers, who is now my husband, also came. Many friends visited me in the hospital. My neighbors helped care for the girls and give them rides when they needed them. When I came home from the hospital, wonderful church friends brought over food, made trips to the grocery store, and even helped clean our house. These were angels in disguise, sent from Heaven. The breast biopsy turned out to be benign. And our dog lived for many more months before we had to put her to sleep.

One of the biggest blessings was finding another job and starting the week after I was cleared for work. This job was everything I wanted and more. It gave me tremendous benefits that I never asked for or knew I needed. And my salary was twice that of my previous position!

I give all the glory to God. These lessons were major milestones in my life where I learned to trust God. As I look back over these times, I can see how He took care of me and my family after my dad died. And the Lord certainly exceeded all my expectations in helping me take care of my girls. Through it all, I never stopped tithing. I gave God the first fruits of my labor and He came through with the rest.

Dear Father,

You are a good and loving Father. Thank you for taking me through these tough lessons to increase my faith and trust in You. There were times when I didn't know if I could make it, but You did. You held my hand, like a father holds his child's hand, and helped me to get through "one day at a time." Just as You fed the Israelites manna in the desert, You fed me and my family. I pray that this story will bear witness to others of Your good and marvelous deeds. I am so grateful to You, Daddy. I promise to never doubt Your faithfulness and providence again.

Hospitals Are Scary Places

I have had my share of scary hospital stays over the years, but none can compare to bringing my daughter, Stephanie, to the hospital. When she was in middle school, she got very sick and had to be hospitalized. Because of her treatment, the doctor did not want a parent to be hanging around the hospital, day and night. I also knew that with my new job and another child to take care of at home, I would not be able to be with her all the time.

After she was admitted, I cried all the way home. I had to entrust the care of my "baby" to the skillful medical professionals. But more importantly, I had to entrust her to God. She went through periods of sadness, loneliness, and anxiety while she was there. I tried the best I could to calm her fears. One thing I taught her was to envision herself in her "happy place." Whether it was a beach, the woods where we hiked, or a bench along a peaceful lake, I asked her to picture herself there and to take time to breathe deeply and soak in the peace of that place. Then I asked her to imagine that she was greeted by a loving, young man with piercing brown eyes. This is Jesus, I said. Let Him hold you and speak words of love and reassurance.

This form of meditation worked not only for her but for me and others. Why does it work? Because we are focusing on the only One who can bring true peace. It says in Scripture, "Come to me all you who are weary and find life burdensome, and I will give you rest." The Father has promised us so many things. This is just one of His many promises. He loves our kids way more than we do. They really belong to Him. They are just on loan to us. He is with each of us 24 hours a day. Sometimes I need to be reminded that I am never alone, just like Stephanie was never alone in the hospital.

As a parent, one of the most important life lessons I taught my kids was about the Father's love and eternal presence. I know that when I sent them off to school or college, God was with them. If they were in the hospital, God was close by. When they moved out of our house and were on their own, God was with them.

Dear Father,
Thank you for the gift of your Word, the Bible. I used to think it was a stuffy old book. It collected dust on the shelf for many years. Now I can't seem to put it down. You knew that Your kids needed something tangible to hold on to, and so You inspired writers to transcribe Your messages into the greatest love letter of all times: the Bible.

When I am scared, the answers to my fright are there. When I am doubting, Your promises are there. When I am confused and need direction, You speak to me through the Bible. When I am tired and anxious and don't know how to pray, Your Word guides and directs me. I thank You that You have rescued me from fear. Whether it's a child in the hospital, losing my job, the death of my parents, or this COVID-19 virus, I have nothing to fear because all Your promises are true.

THE LATER YEARS

LETTERS FROM 5 YEARS AGO TO THE PRESENT

College and young adulthood

I always thought that once my kids were out of college, parenting would get easier. Not true. Unfortunately, the scars of divorce on the girls and my step-son were not yet healed. We were trying to blend our family. Each adult child had unique challenges in college and after. Launching on their own was marked with ups and downs. They moved back into the house for a time, and so the interactions and rules were different. They changed jobs and relationships. Parenting adult children has been a lesson in patience and learning when to keep silent. It is also a tremendous time of personal and spiritual growth. This has been my favorite Bible verse for this time:

Philippians 4:13 "I can do all things through Christ, Who strengthens me."

Break My Heart for What Breaks Yours

There is a song that I love called “Hosanna.” There is one line that resonates with me: "Break my heart for what breaks Yours." I always wondered what that meant and why I wanted my heart to break like Your Father’s heart breaks. Now I know. The closer we get to the Father, the more intimate we are to share in His feelings.

I used to think that my heart has been broken so many times that nothing else could hurt as much as the hurts from the past. Broken relationships with boyfriends, friends that betrayed me, disappointments at school and work, infertility, being misunderstood, a broken marriage, the death of both of my parents. Could anything hurt my heart more?

Sadly, the answer was yes. My oldest daughter, the mother of little Gwen, severed ties with us and barred us from having any contact with her. Days evolved into weeks. Weeks evolved into months. Now almost six years have gone by since I've seen my daughter and our little Gwen. I even have a second granddaughter, Charlotte, whom I’ve never met. She was even born on my birthday.

All of our kids have hurt and disappointed us at one time or another, but I haven't experienced the targeted hate that I have had from our daughter. I can't believe that somebody that I love so much could ever be so mean to me. I never knew that this kind of rejection could hurt my heart so much! I realize that we all have free will and that she is just exercising hers. When she exercised her free will to our favor, it was marvelous. When it was against us, how it hurts.

Dear Father,

I am so sorry for the times that exercising my free will has hurt others — but most of all — You. I can't even imagine how You continue to love me even though I have hurt Your heart so badly. In spite of every sin I committed, You keep on loving me. You are amazing, Father! Thank you for showing how Your heart breaks every time I walked away from You. When I multiply that wound of my sins by the millions of sins committed every day, I can't even imagine what that hurt must feel like for You. Keep breaking my heart for what breaks Yours, so I never take your love and forgiveness for granted.

Heal my heart and make it clean
Open up my eyes to the things unseen
Show me how to love like you have loved me
Break my heart for what breaks yours
Everything I am for your kingdom's cause
As I walk from earth into eternity.
© Hillsong

Happy Birthday?

Five years ago, our oldest daughter severed ties with us. The pain of that rejection is so deep. We have tried everything to reconcile with her, but she still has a wall up. To add salt to the wound, she has a relationship with her birthmother and step-mom, which she flaunts for all to see. And yet, I am her "real" mother. "What about me, Rachel?" I often ask. "When will you remember your mother and come back to me?"

Today Rachel turned 30. I will not be joining in any of the celebrations as she passes from her 20s into her 30s. She has been our pride and joy for the past 25 years. We adopted her when she was only 11 weeks old. I always hoped that I would be able to celebrate all of the birthdays and major holidays with our kids. We never really knew anyone who had children that divorced their parents. Imagine the shock and disappointment when this parent/child divorce happened to us!

Missing her milestone birthday was one of several disappointments. Earlier this year, there were two more cracks in the wall of disappointment. We saw Rachel and our two granddaughters, at events for our daughter, Stephanie. What a joy it was to spend a few hours with the three of them, even though Rachel was distant. I have missed SO much of her life these past five years, not to mention missing our granddaughters' childhoods. How ironic that Charlotte was born on MY birthday. God certainly has a unique way of reminding Rachel that she has a mom, even if she chooses to distance herself from me.

None of us can live life without experiencing pain and rejection. There are all sorts of rejection caused by circumstances beyond our control.

Today, when I want to see our daughter on this special day, I am trying NOT to focus on the pain inside. I am trying to battle the negative thoughts in my head. Instead of dwelling in the sea of pity and negativity, I am standing on God's Word. In fact, I am calling on many Bible verses to give me comfort and peace, on a day when the enemy wants to remind me that I will not see or talk to my Rachel.

> *Joel 2:25 – I will repay you for the years, which the locust has eaten.*
> *Nehemiah 13-2 – God turned the curse into a blessing!*
> *Jeremiah 32:27 – I am the Lord God of all man. Is there anything impossible to me?*

I don't know when or if this will be resolved, but I know that I have to have faith, because without faith, it is impossible to please God. (Hebrews 11:6).

Dear Father,
I know that I have rejected You too. I can't imagine the pain you feel each and every day when we reject You. You are the perfect parent. You are true love. You have a heart so big and full of mercy and love and desire to wrap me up in it, like a cozy blanket. Today Father, help me to keep my mind on all that is pure and holy and true. Guard my heart and mind from the fiery darts of the enemy. Fill me with Your joy and peace. Thank you for loving me so much and for giving me Rachel 30 years ago today! I have had so many blessings of motherhood -- too many to count. Thank you, Father, for blessing me the way that only YOU know how to do.

Heart Pain

Some days, the weight of not seeing Gwen, Charlotte, and Rachel is too much for me to bear. There are days when I look forward to seeing Gwen, when she is with her dad, and then something would come up and the schedule would change. I actually feel physical pain in my heart when I don't get to spend time with my children, Rachel and Stephanie. I know that as teenagers, they have their own lives, but I still miss our times together.

Father, is this how Your heart hurts when we don't spend enough time with You? Am I being too sensitive? Or am I right where I am supposed to be?

After a year and a half of pursuing my daughter and trying to meet to talk about what's bothering her, I finally decided to file a petition in family court for visitation of Gwen (she was the only granddaughter at the time). I really hated to take this step, but I didn't know what else to do. One of the hardest things I ever had to do was to write one more email, asking to get together with her and Gwen. If I didn't hear from her by a certain date, I was going to move forward with my plans for filing papers in court.

The morning came when I headed to court. As I drove downtown to the courthouse, my hands shook, and my eyes started to water. I couldn't believe that I was at this point. My own daughter was forcing me to take an action I didn't want to take. Why did this have to be the only way for a grandparent to see a grandchild? It felt so wrong.

I sat outside of the courthouse for a while. Would she pick up if I called her one last time? It was her lunch hour. I dialed and prayed that she would answer. If only she reached out to me, I would drop everything and run to meet with her. I would drop the court thing too. So, I dialed and I waited, just like the Father would have done. (You see, God always gives us one more chance before He moves.) No answer. She didn't pick up. How sad and heartbreaking. I approached the courthouse. My whole body was shaking. I could hardly swallow. There was a huge lump in my throat. Tears welled up in my eyes as I walked through security and into the courthouse. I dropped off the papers[1], walked out to my car and unlocked the door. I sat in my car and just cried and cried! Why did it have to get to this point? Why couldn't she meet with me? Why wasn't she talking to me? What did I do to deserve this treatment? And then I remembered the line from the song, "Break my heart for what breaks Yours." Wow! Another chance to feel Your pain.

Dear Father,
It says in Your word, "In all things give thanks." Really? Do I really need to give You thanks when my heart is breaking like this? Do I need to be merciful like You are merciful? I do if I want to be one of Your followers. I do, Father, especially if I pray, "break my heart for what breaks Yours." Help me Father, to grow closer to You, especially when my heart is breaking. Forgive me for all the times I have broken Your heart. You certainly don't deserve it. You are so loving and kind, even when we don't treat You this way.

---

[1] The court had us appear in court with Rachel and her ex. We did not win our case.

Agony in the Garden

Today was "one of those awful days." My mind kept drifting back to missing Gwen and Rachel. The pain I have been feeling is all around my heart. When I am low, like today, sometimes I head down the slippery slope of going even lower. My thoughts go from optimistic, to sad, to worried, to despair, to the pits — just in a second.

Then I travel into the awful room of "What ifs." What if she never does come around? What if her heart stays hardened forever? What if she carries this grudge into the next decade, and the next one, and the one after that? How old will I be then? How many years will we have lost? What if Gwen gets really messed up with all that's going on? What if Gwen forgets her Grammy and her Papa? What if Gwen's memories of us become so faint that she never looks us up? What if after all I do, this situation never turns around? What if I never get to meet our granddaughter, Charlotte? Will Gwen at least tell her sister about us? What if Charlotte never looks us up?

I still love Rachel and I would take her back in a second. She's my daughter and you never stop loving your kids, right Father? I choose to forgive her and be in relationship again. Even with my broken heart, I STILL want to spend time with her, now and forever.

And then the thought entered my head; "I wonder if this is part (or maybe most) of the agony that Jesus felt in the Garden of Gethsemane?" Physical pain is one thing, and You know I have had my share of that; but the emotional pain — that tears your heart apart and ties your stomach in knots — is quite another.

I can’t even imagine the emotional pain Your Son must have felt in the garden. In spite of all He did for all of His children, people would still be lost and unsaved. In spite of His everlasting love, they would still turn away from Him and keep going down the road that leads to death and destruction. How heart wrenching it must have been for Jesus to think about this, the hour before the arrest.

In the Garden, did Jesus see all the faces of those who would never come around to salvation? Did the emotional weight of losing so many to Satan just break His heart? No wonder He cried and sweated blood. He knew who those souls would be. And the thought of never being able to spend eternity with them was just too much to bear. Emotional pain is so intense that it feels like you're buried under thousands of pounds of bricks and can't get up. It's dark in this place and it hurts. Oh, does it hurt! The greater Your love, the deeper the pain must have been!

I know that You love each of us as if there was only one of us. It is so hard for me to imagine a love like this, but You do! Are You done “breaking my heart for what breaks Yours?

Dear Father,
Thank you for giving me a brief glimpse into the Garden. Thank you for sharing Your broken heart with me. I had never known this before. I pray that I will never take Your love and sacrifice for granted. When I whine, help me to shut my mouth and keep the focus on all You have done for me. Take my prayers and tears and use them to bring more souls to You. Give me Your eyes to see those in my life that still need salvation, who need You, and help me to pray for them even more.

Just like I can't bear the thought of not reconciling with Rachel and not ever spending time with her, it must hurt You so much more! When You multiply this pain by all the souls that are lost now and will be lost forever, how can You stand it? Wow! Thank you, Father, that we are all Your kids and You want to be with us FOREVER. If there is any small part You want me to play to bring more souls to you, use me. I'm all in.

"Happy" Mother's Day 2016

Parenting is a wild roller coaster ride of ups and downs. Not all parenting experiences are happy. This one is an especially painful example. I wrote this letter in 2016 when I flew up to Albany to surprise my youngest daughter, Stephanie, on Mother's Day. At this point, our oldest daughter still was not in relationship with us.

I had breakfast with Stephanie before she went off to spend the holiday with her sister, Rachel, her dad (my ex) and his wife (her step-mom). While I was grateful that I got to see Stephanie at breakfast, I felt rejected and alone on Mother's Day. I was 1,500 miles from my husband and home in Florida. I was by myself on a day that the rest of the country celebrates motherhood. After spending my life for these two girls, I was in our hometown and there was no room for me at their Mother's Day Brunch. As if that rejection wasn't enough, I was grieving that Rachel still wasn't talking to me.

Dear adopted daughter of mine,

This Mother's Day will be like the last one and the one before that and the one before that and the one before that. I will not hear from you, again. You will spend it with your daughters and your step-mother and most likely, you will call your birth mother.

You will never realize how much this breaks my heart until your daughters ignore you on Mother's Day, your birthday, Thanksgiving, and Christmas. All of the holidays that I always treasured by celebrating with my kids, I am alone.

I don't know why it has to be this way. I made a conscious choice to adopt you and give you a better life than you would have had if your birthmother tried to raise you. I was the one who walked the floors at night when you were sick. I watched you take your first steps and say your first words. I took you to church and raised you in the Christian faith. I have never stopped praying for you!

I went to every program you ever had at school, even into your four years of college. I sacrificed my own career to stay at home with you, so you and your sister wouldn't be latch-key kids. When you needed braces, or new shoes for sports, or a new dress for a dance, I put my own shopping desires aside, so I could buy you what you wanted or needed. Living on one income wasn't easy when your dad I and became divorced.

Each birthday of yours was planned and orchestrated, with a different theme, so it would be extra special, just like you. I enjoyed traveling with you and even flew out to California to meet your birthmother when you were in elementary school. This was a closed adoption until I decided to open it up by searching for your birthmother. I thought this would be best for you and for her.

I watched you graduate from high school and then watched you get whisked away by your birth family, while your dad and I walked to our cars in tears, our heads hanging down, wondering what just happened. This truly was one of the biggest slaps in the face from your birth family. Why weren't <u>your parents</u> invited to your high school graduation celebration? After all, we had the unexpected expense of private high school, not to mention everything else that went with being a supportive parent. We decided that it was best for you to go to private school and so we sacrificed.

I was there for your four years of college and spent down my savings so that you could reach your dream. Do you remember how I was there in Daytona Beach to watch you and your U-Albany team compete in the national cheerleading competition? There wasn't any distance I wouldn't go to support you and build you up.

When you became pregnant your junior year of college, I stood by you and encouraged you throughout your pregnancy and schoolwork, so you wouldn't drop out of college. I even went to your maternity appointments with you. And when you gave birth to Gwen, I was right there in the waiting room, anticipating the first look at my legacy, my 1st grandchild. I rearranged my work schedule, and almost lost my job, so I could babysit so you could go to class.

I helped plan and paid for your wedding and watched Gwen, so you could honeymoon for a week. I helped you move into countless apartments and even into our home with Gwen when your marriage fell apart. And when you hooked up with a boyfriend who wasn't so good for you, I took a huge risk and told you of my concern. That was over five years and I am still paying the price by not seeing you or my granddaughters.

So, my dear, on this Mother's Day, while you are still hanging on to resentment, unforgiveness, and hate, I am hanging on to 20-some years of memories of a life that I lived, the best that I could. I am hanging on to love, when I want to hate you for how you have broken my heart. I am hanging on to peace, when I want to rage at how your actions towards me have hurt your girls. I am hanging on to hope instead of despair, that someday you will reconcile before it's too late. And I am hanging on to the future, instead of looking back.

Happy Mother's Day, Rachel.

With love from your imperfect, but loving, Mom

Dear Father,

Because you see and know ALL things, I wrote this letter but never sent it. As I reread this letter, I can still feel the excruciating pain in my heart that Mother's Day. Does Your heart ever hurt like that? There were so many times when I ignored you. When I didn't speak to You for days and weeks on end. When I was being rebellious and living in sin, I pulled away from You. Did this hurt you, Father? There were times when I was so mad at You, I wanted to forget you altogether.

Then, when I decided to come back to You, I was ashamed. I was sorry for putting you through this pain of ignoring You. I was afraid to come back to You too. I feared judgement and punishment. I even feared eternal damnation because I thought my sins were so bad.

But I remembered that You are pure love. I don't know how I remembered this when I was so mixed up. I can't believe that You kept on loving me when I messed up or got angry with you. During all of these ugly seasons of my life, You were patient and kind to me. There wasn't a day or a minute that went by when You weren't keeping Your eye on me. And when I realized my sinfulness, You welcomed me back in a heartbeat. No judgement. No condemnation. Just open arms, patiently waiting for me to come back to You.

Not only did You hold me close to Your heart, You even whispered words of love in my ear. You held me on Your lap while I cried and cried. And You showered me with blessings! Unexpected blessings that I didn't deserve. What kind of parent does this? What kind of Father loves his kids like this? Only You. Only You!

1 Chronicles 16:34 (NIV) Oh, give thanks to the Lord, for He is good! For His love endures forever.

Thank you, Father, for walking next to me during one of the most painful experiences in my life. Thank you for Your promises and for the family and friends that accompanied me on this painful journey. Thank you for putting angels in my life to remind me of Your love. You allowed me to live out the story of the Prodigal Son from all sides. Thank you for equipping me to help others in this same situation.

Joy Comes in the Morning

It says in scripture, those who sow with tears will reap with songs joy (Psalm 126:5). I often ask myself how I can have any joy when I am going through this separation from Rachel and the girls. It seems that all the holidays, especially Mother's Day, our birthdays, and Christmas have a black cloud hanging over them. It's hard to be joyful or thankful when I am in so much pain.

One way the Father directed my steps during this time was to think about other kids who could benefit from a loving grandma and grandpa. Evelyn is a little girl who lives next door. Her grandparents live in Canada most of the year and are only in Florida part-time. When they are back in Canada, we are like her surrogate grandparents. We love her to pieces. The Lord also brought other friends' children into our lives here in Florida: Brooks and Maddi, Caleb and Claire, Steven and his sister, Andrea.

Recently, we were at a Christian concert and heard about Compassion International. This international organization allows people to sponsor a child from a foreign country. For a modest donation every month, we sponsor a little girl in East Indonesia, who is the same age as our Gwen. She receives medical checkups, food assistance, tutoring for school, and emotional support. She also receives Christian religious education. I may not be able to see Gwen, but I can interact with Chelsey through cards and letters. Compassion has a staff that translates the letters into her language and her letters to us in English. It is amazing that whenever I am feeling the most depressed, a letter from Chelsey arrives in the mail. What a way that the Lord uses to comfort me.

A few years after we sponsored Chelsey, we found another child, this time in the Dominican Republic (DR). Her name is Scarlett, and she is Charlotte's age. We have corresponded several times and we have grown to really love each other. In January 2019, I was blessed to go on a mission trip to the DR and meet Scarlett, her mom, and her Compassion worker. My heart melted when she ran into my arms. We swam, shared stories about our families, and put a puzzle of the United States together. We had a beautiful lunch and spent time in the afternoon opening the gifts I brought. When it was time for Scarlett to go home, she hugged me and cried. I cried too. I marveled at the bond we felt through all our letters and this one visit. This was clearly a God-ordained blessing.

I was able to encourage her to do well in school and be obedient to her parents. More importantly, I encouraged her to pray and stay close to Jesus. She asked me when I was coming back to see her and if I could also bring my family. She wants us to attend her high school graduation, her college graduation, and even her wedding! Even though she was only in second grade when we met, she certainly has big dreams ahead. This is how Compassion International works to lift children out of poverty. The sponsors are a big part of the equation.

Dear Father,
I am so grateful that You had these creative ideas for us to unite with these precious children. Even though my heart is breaking because I can't see my daughter and her girls, You have found a way to have me show Your love. I am so blessed, Father to be on the receiving end of love too. I love that you value children so much that You want them to be protected and thrive. And You want us to be more like them. Thank you

for Compassion and other ministries like this that connect us with needy children from around the world. Even here, Father, help Your children thrive with love and attention. Thank you for bringing our friends' kids into my life, to enjoy and love, even when I can't see some of my own grandchildren.

A Taste of Reconciliation

I don't know what's worse, to have a taste of reconciliation with someone or no contact at all. Four months ago, I got to see my daughter, Rachel, and meet my 3-year-old granddaughter, Charlotte, for the first time. I also got to see Gwen, who is now eight. Although Rachel and Charlotte were very distant and cautious, they were polite. Gwen, on the other hand, came running into my arms and said, "Oh, Grandma, how I missed you!"

It was a very emotional reunion, but I had to keep my mouth and thoughts in check because we were really there for my grandson's second birthday party. No one wanted to exchange any more than pleasantries since we were in a public place with lots of people there. I was extremely grateful for this first step towards reconciliation. There was a glimmer of hope at the end of the party when we took a family picture. Rachel and our two granddaughters were in it.

I wanted to hang on to this moment for as long as I could. I didn't know if and when I would ever see them again. While I still can't fathom how a person can hang on to anger and unforgiveness for five plus years and do things to hurt her children and her mom, I couldn't let my mind go there. All I did was love my daughter unconditionally and turn this over in prayer.

Dear Father,

It must hurt Your heart so much when we come close and then turn away. You love each person as if we were an only child. I can't even imagine how to always love unconditionally like You do. I know that all You want to do is spend time with me and have an intimate relationship, but there have been times in my life when I have walked completely away from You. How that must have hurt!

And still, I think of Your forgiveness and how You welcomed me back each and every time. What a gift of divine mercy. I only pray that I can be this way with Rachel. Love. Forgive. Be merciful. Do not judge. I sure need a lot of grace, each and every day, to make this happen.

The Prodigal Returns

There is a poignant story in the Bible about a son who left home with his inheritance. His father was distraught about his son leaving home, but the father did nothing to stop him. While that son was away, the father stayed on the farm and worked with his other son. One day, the son who left home, ran out of money and was living with the pigs. He realized the error of his ways and came crawling back home. While this son was far off, his father saw him and ran to greet him. He fully expected his father to be angry with him and let him live in the barn with the animals. Instead, the father wept tears of joy to have his son back again. The grateful father threw him a party and gave his son a new robe and ring. Meanwhile, the other son, who had been faithful and loyal to his dad, saw what was happening and was jealous. Why did his brother get all the gifts and attention?

For many years, I related to this story only from the prodigal son's perspective. I had been a wild child when I was a teen and disappointed my parents and certainly God. When I changed my ways and came crawling back to the Father, He welcomed me with open arms.

The experience with Rachel led me to relate to the father in this story. What was that father doing when the son was away? He was, most likely, working, praying, and focusing on the relationships around him, such as his other son. I found great wisdom from meditating on the father in this story. By keeping the focus on God and also on the things I could control, I was able to navigate a very difficult period. I also prayed that if and when Rachel wanted to come back, I would be open and forgiving, as the father in this story.

Then I wondered, if there was a reunion, how would our two other children react? For six years, we grew even closer to Stephanie and Greg. We rejoiced when Stephanie had her two boys and we partied when Greg got married. When Greg and Xu had their first baby, Stone, it was another celebration. For six years, they had our full attention. With Rachel, Gwen, and Charlotte back in the picture, would they be jealous?

I believe that this story came to life in our own family. The six years without Rachel were so difficult. Not only did we miss her, we also missed seeing Gwen grow up. She was four and in pre-kindergarten when Rachel left. During the time she was gone, she also had another baby, Charlotte, who was born on my birthday! I didn't get to be part of her pregnancy, like I was with her firstborn. I never got to hold Charlotte as a baby or celebrate her first three birthdays. I didn't get to meet Charlotte until she was almost three. When I think of all the missed milestones in their lives, I feel cheated. I could just cry, and often, I did. But that was not the end of the story.

When I learned that Rachel actually wanted to see us, I could not believe it. I was skeptical. I guarded my heart so I wouldn't suffer any more should she change her mind. I longed to be reunited, and so I took a chance. We began with a long distance phone call. And then another call. We planned to see her a few weeks later when we went traveled to Albany. Conscious that something could still go wrong, I was fearful and guarded. I tried not to get my hopes up, as I had been hurt so many times before.

Thankfully, we had a joyous reunion with Rachel and the girls. We were able to plan a party with Rachel and her girls, together with Stephanie and her boys, Owen and Daniel. What a great reunion!

I am grateful that we have worked through the issues that separated us. I now have a great relationship with Rachel and her girls. I had to work through some jealousy issues with our other daughter and I always have to be aware of their feelings. I cannot play favorites. The Lord clearly has done great things for us and we are filled with joy (Psalm 126:3)

Dear Father,
Thank you for sustaining me through those years. Thank you for hearing our prayers for a reunion and the grace to orchestrate it. You have taught me so much about unconditional love and forgiveness through this experience and I am grateful. I was warned during those years that I could either become better or become bitter. I am happy that I did not grow bitter. It would have been so easy to do. Thank you for giving me a glimpse of the joy in Your heart when one of us returns to You. Even when we hurt You so much, You never stop loving us. You are truly an amazing parent.

Don't You Dare Criticize Her

All of my kids have done things that make me cringe. After all, nobody is perfect. I remember an incident where one of my kids went off the deep end and did something I could never have imagined. If you are a parent, you know what I mean. While I was shocked, disappointed, angry, and embarrassed, I also never stopped loving that child.

After the incident, the comments came flooding in from other people. Relatives and friends, who have never even had kids, were the biggest critics of all. I was so upset when others started to bad-mouth my child. It's bad enough when I was thinking these thoughts, but hearing other people spew judgement and bad names really made me angry.

Just think of how our Father must feel when we mess` up. We ALL have done things we were embarrassed about. Things that were sinful. Things that resulted in shame and heaps of guilt. But instead of our Father looking at us and saying, "Boy, what a screw up this person is. She will never amount to much. What was she thinking when she did that? That's not how I raised her," God graciously shows us mercy, forgiveness, and unconditional love. He not only forgives our sins, but He forgets. What a role model for me as a mom!

How do you think the Father feels when we talk negatively about one another? Words kill. (Proverbs 18:21) They not only kill the heart, but they destroy a person's reputation. When we are judgmental of one another, that must feel like a knife in His heart. Worst of all, when we judge and condemn His Bride, the Church, by being critical of pastors, staff, other denominations, etc., it must be so hard for Him to hold back His anger.

Do you ever wonder what the world would be like if everyone was filled with forgiveness and unconditional love? What would it be like if everyone read the story of the prodigal son in the Bible and then walked it out with family and friends?

Dear Father,
I have sinned so many times. I have done stupid things that have brought on shame and guilt. And yet, You take me back. Your unconditional love is amazing. I can't even fathom the fact that while we were yet sinners, and even before we were born, you KNEW that we needed a Savior. You are the One who redeems us and restores us back into Your family. Thank you for Your Son, Jesus, who took the punishment that I deserved for my sins, by dying a horrible death on the cross. Let me NEVER take this gift of salvation for granted. Give me the courage to share all that You have done for ME to others. Keep me from being judgmental and angry. Show me how to love well.

Death – Oh Where Is Your Sting?

On Sunday, my good friend from Albany called to deliver the most shocking and sad news. She found her daughter dead in her apartment! Having not seen her daughter in three months, as my friend spends the winter in Florida, she was looking forward to this reunion. The morning that she was going to meet her daughter for brunch, she went to her daughter's apartment because she couldn't reach her. How traumatic to lose a child, let alone be the one who discovered her sudden death!

I have often thought of this scenario happening to me. I always prayed that Rachel and I would become reconciled before it was too late. Having buried my parents, numerous friends, and other close relatives, I know how fragile and fleeting life is. None of us knows the day or the hour when we will be called home.

Dear Father,

I pray for my friend and all the mothers in the world who have had to bury a child. This is not the right order of things. We always expect to die before our children. And yet, for so many people, this is what happens. I pray that You will shower them with grace to get through these experiences and the courage to move forward with their lives. Please heal their broken hearts. Bring those who don't know Your Son into the knowledge of Him. I ask for an increase of faith and hope when planning for what is to come and the courage to tell others about the free gift of salvation through your Son. I know from experience, that saying yes to Your Son is the only assurance that I will join those I love in Heaven one day.

The Mystery of Free Will

Raising kids is hard work. A wise friend once told me, "Little kids… little problems. Big kids… big problems." Today was one of those days. Even though we live 1,500 miles away from our three grown kids, we are in touch all the time. Sometimes, I know too much of their business. The constant challenge I have is to keep my mouth shut and mind my own business. Parents, does this sound familiar?

When they were small, we got to make the decisions for them. Now it's their turn to make their own. I have a hard time watching them make choices that will end up in heartache for them and/or their kids. When I see them hurting and I know that it is a direct result of a poor choice they made, I have to exert a Herculean amount of self-control to try not to "fix it" for them. I also go back and forth with the question, "Is my involvement helping or hurting? Am I really helping, or am I enabling them to stay stuck in their situation?" Often, the situation I see is too painful and I need to look the other way and respect their choices, even if it kills me.

This is where the "mystery" of free will comes in. I call it a mystery because it makes no sense to me. I often wonder why God gave us free will, when so often, our free will ends up hurting ourselves or others. As a mother of adult children, all I can really do is listen, pray, and be supportive. I can't live their lives for them. I can't manage their money or their careers. I can't offer unsolicited advice. I have to practice acceptance with their choices, as difficult as that may be.

Dear Father,

Today I need to hear the whisper of Your voice that everything will be alright with my children and grandchildren. I need Your reassurance that You are in control of the universe at all times, and that You don't need any help from me to make the world go 'round. I pray for Your peace that surpasses all understanding as I do life with my adult children. Please give me the wisdom to know what to say and what not to say. When is the time to help and when is it better to pull back? Give me the understanding of Your perfect will in all things, especially when it comes to the relationships with my adult children and their families. It's so hard, Father. It's hard to watch my kids or grandkids suffer and realize that I am powerless to change anything in their lives.

How do You feel when You watch me make choices that hurt myself or even others? What must it be like to be the Father of over 7 billion people, all at once, and know every small detail about each one of us? You truly are amazing, Father.

The Cycle of Life

When my kids were small, they ran to me with every problem they had. Big or small, they brought problems to me or their dad. As they got older, this happened less and less. By the time they were in high school, they rarely came to me with most problems. I only got the super huge problems. They talked to their friends before they confided in me. This was the age where "I don't need your help and parents are stupid."

As they got older, into their twenties, and on their own, there was a slow shift back to me for advice. When each of the girls had a baby of their own, they were more open about sharing their challenges. Our grown son.... not so much. He and his wife seemed to have all the answers about parenting and work/life balance and didn't want us to interfere.

This pattern of sharing and closeness is similar to the stages of my relationship with God the Father. When I was a new believer, I was very close to Him and shared everything. After time, I drifted and relied more on friends, self-help books, and TV talk shows to get information and solve problems. Often, I would pick up the phone and talk to a friend or family member before I shared with the Lord. With time and age, I am drawing nearer to God. I realize that God's wisdom and guidance is far superior to anyone else.

Dear Father,
Help me to know how to parent my adult children. They are at an age where they want to be independent, yet they still struggle with relationships, child rearing, work, and money issues. Help me to point them to You and give them the grace to see that You have their best

interest in mind. You are the only source of perfect wisdom. You have the correct answer to any problem. Give my adult children the eyes to see who You really are and the role You want to play in their lives.

WHAT I LEARNED FROM WRITING THIS BOOK

I received many blessings and revelations in the process of compiling these stories. I learned about God's nature and how He wants to have an intimate relationship with us. As my relationship with the Father grew, He kept showing me the treasures in His heart. I learned why the Father wants us to imitate a child. The parent-child relationship is sacred and teaches us so much, if we only take the time. Remember how you were when you gazed into a baby's eyes for the first time? The love. The promise. The awe. That's how our Father looks at you, His precious creation. Lastly, I had a deeper understanding of what it means to be adopted into God's family.

GOD'S NATURE

First, we will never know everything about God's nature. It is so vast and complicated. He exceeds every image we may have of Him. His wisdom, creativity, intelligence, compassion, mercy, and love far surpass our imagination. There are not enough words in our dictionary to adequately describe Him.

Before I started this book, I had a very distorted view of God's character and nature. It was partially because of my upbringing, the church I was attending, and my interaction with other people. Over time, I learned the truth of who He really is.

I believe that all He revealed to me through Scripture, combined with a personal relationship with His son, Jesus, has changed my life. I went from a scared kid to a confident daughter. He added more revelation through the gifts of parenting and adoption. This was an unexpected blessing I received when I adopted Rachel and then Stephanie.

As my relationship with Him grows deeper, He shows me more of who He is. This first-hand experience has been invaluable to my understanding of Him as the perfect parent. In this process, He taught me so much about parenting my kids and relating to them now that they are adults. He touches my heart when I discover the feelings I have for my kids. His love for us is far different than the love we have toward our kids. It's a million times greater!

Here is a glimpse of some of His attributes. Many of them are spelled out in Psalm 103. As you dive into Scripture, you will find many more.

- Forgiving – When we repent, He not only forgives us, He forgets our sins.
- Protector – When we call on Him for protection, of any kind, He always delivers according to His perfect will.
- Pleased – He is thrilled when we obey Him and when we use the gifts He gave us.
- Encouraging – In a world that tries to tear us down, He is our strongest encourager. He is our cheerleader, not our critic.
- Patient – He receives us back after we have strayed far from Him. He stands back and lets us learn lessons the hard way, instead of intervening.
- Generous – every good gift comes from above. His generosity is infinite.

- Wise – He and His word, the Bible, are vast storehouses of wisdom. He longs to share His eternal perspective and knowledge with us.
- Great listener – He is available to us 24/7. He never turns a deaf ear to our cries.
- Supportive – He always has our best interest in mind. He has our back, forever and always.
- Filled with grace – When we deserve punishment, He gives us divine favor.
- Wonderful guide – He guides us in the right direction. He sometimes does this by saying "no" to our prayers. He lets us learn from our mistakes.
- Helper – As the creator of the universe, He is the best one to go to with questions.
- Healer – I have been the recipient of so many divine healings. He wants to see us healed and whole. The healings that Jesus did in His lifetime, were only the beginning to show us the healing power of the Father.
- Creative – The Father transforms us into a new creation when we accept His Son, Jesus. Just look back on the person you used to be and the person you have become since Jesus entered your life. He is constantly recreating us, making us more like His Son.
- Lover – He loves His children equally. He plays no favorites. His love is without end.

BE CHILDLIKE

It says in Scripture that unless we become like a little child, we will not enter the kingdom of Heaven. *"Truly I tell you, unless you change and become like little children, you will never enter the kingdom of heaven." Matthew 18:3* What does it mean to be like a child? Some of the qualities of infants and children include:

- Humble – asking the parent or elder for help
- Trusting – that parents will provide for them and take care of them
- Accepting – of people and situations
- Always learning – new things, learning from mistakes
- Curious – always looking for answers
- Filled with joy and laughter
- Unworried
- Live in the present
- Loving and affectionate
- Playful

Scripture never said to be childish, in fact, the Father wants us to grow in our relationship with Him. He wants us to stop acting so childish when we should be acting like a mature Christian. He wants us to "go deeper" with Him and not just be fed milk all the time. 1 Peter 2:2 – *"Like newborn babies, crave pure spiritual milk, so that by it you may grow up in your salvation."* In other words, He wants us to grow up and become a disciple maker, not a person who is always looking to be fed. He wants us to be giving, instead of being selfish and always asking, "What's in it for me."

MIRACLE OF ADOPTION

It says in Scripture that when we accept Jesus as our Lord and Savior, we become adopted sons and daughters of God. We become part of His family, forever. What great news! *"Because you are His sons, God sent the Spirit of His son into our hearts, the Spirit who calls out 'Abba, Father.' So, you are no longer a slave, but God's child; and since you are His child, God has made you also an heir." Galatians 4:6-7*

I thought about this in light of adopting our two daughters. Our adoption in court, was a binding, legal document, which both parents had to sign. It portrayed a covenant relationship with each daughter. This covenant meant that each girl would receive our name. They became part of our permanent family and our extended family. Our wealth would be shared with them as we provided for their every need. Our girls are our legacy. *"He provides food for those who fear him; he remembers his covenant forever." (Psalm 111:5)* God believes in establishing covenants with His people. His adopted sons and daughters are bound by a covenant with Him. The same is true with our adoption.

Just like we were glad to share everything with the girls, now that they are in our family, so the Father wants to share everything in His kingdom with us. It says in Luke 12:32, *"Do not be afraid, little flock, for your Father has been pleased to give you the kingdom."*

EPILOGUE

Matthew 7:7-11 "Ask, and it will be given to you; seek, and you will find; knock, and it will be opened to you. For everyone who asks receives, and he who seeks finds, and to him who knocks it will be opened. Or what man is there among you who, if his son asks for bread, will give him a stone? Or if he asks for a fish, will he give him a serpent? If you then, being evil, know how to give good gifts to your children, how much more will your Father who is in heaven give good things to those who ask Him."

Family relationships are dynamic. Thank God for that! We can hope and trust that whatever situation we are in will change. Too often when I was going through a painful season, I would slip into depression and begin to believe that things were always going to be this way. If this is you, I urge you to talk to your pastor, a Christian counselor, or a trusted friend who has faith in Christ. The negative talk, I learned the hard way, was the voice of the enemy. Since he couldn't accuse me before the Father's throne, because of what Jesus did for me, he came directly at me. A fellow Christ follower can pray for you and help to pull you out of the pit of despair and depression. I am thankful for the team that helped me.

The story of our family continues. Many of the painful situations in this book have been resolved. The six-year separation, from our daughter and two granddaughters, has been resolved. It began when my daughter wanted to see me the next time we came to town. We had several long phone conversations beforehand. Our first gathering was a birthday party for our oldest granddaughter. Our other daughter also came with her son. We had a beautiful time.

Since then, we have had many visits, holiday celebrations, and family reunions. We even had a Disney trip with my daughter, Rachel, and her two girls. In the story of the prodigal son in the Bible, the parent gave the son a ring and a robe for a homecoming present. In my case, it was a Disney trip.

I am so thankful to the Father for opening this door for me and our family. We also have had two family reunions with all three children and their families. These reunions have been the highlight of each of the past two years.

Even during the hardest times, I always believed that God is good. His nature never changes. He is the same yesterday, today, and tomorrow. Though our circumstances may change, we can always seek the Father. He loves when we do that. He waits to comfort and bless us. Like it says in Matthew 7:7-11 Scripture, when we seek Him, we will find Him. When we ask, we will receive. And when we knock, our Father always opens the door. May you be blessed today and may your love for the Father grow each day, until He welcomes you into His arms.

ACKNOWLEDGEMENTS

I am grateful to my husband, Rick, who has been my biggest cheerleader for this project. He has prayed with me, coached me, and motivated me when I didn't think I could finish this project. My adopted mother, Sr. Mary Clare, walked beside me as I did this entire project. She was a champion of this book and gave me the courage to believe in it too, when I had trouble believing in myself. Sadly, she passed away on March 28, 2020 (during the COVID-19 pandemic), before this book was published.

I would like to thank my trusty team of reviewers, who shared their insight and offered editorial comments: Annette Brooks, Zoe Alexander Ruwoldt, Diane Hemphill, Karen West, and Carol Theilen. These women are also my prayer partners and dear sisters in Christ. I also thank my youngest brother, Anthony Zerucha, and Fr. George Brucker for keeping me in constant prayer, for reviewing the manuscript, and for sharing valuable insights.

A special thanks to Shiloh and Justin Williams, who graciously agreed to be on the cover of my book. The love and awe that Shiloh, age three, has her for her daddy was captured by my photographer husband, Rick. I thank Nikki Williams for her assistance the day of the photo shoot.

Lastly, I would like to thank David Wagner from Father's Heart Ministries, who reviewed this manuscript and encouraged me to publish a book that reveals the heart of the Father towards His children. David's prophetic gifting empowered me to discover my destiny, as a Christian author, and rediscover my identity in Christ.

AUTHOR'S BACKGROUND

Service in God's family is taught, not caught. From an early age, I witnessed my parents and grandparents mentoring, helping, praying, and volunteering in church and community. I started family ministry in my 20s, helping infertile and then adoptive couples through the most difficult time of their lives. Through my own experience, I also coached step-families, trying to blend two families into one.

Prayer and fellowship were the cornerstone for all the ministry assignments through the years. When my kids were young, I started the Holy Family Prayer Group for families with young kids. We met weekly for years and created bonds that have never been broken. I also served in youth ministry (Grades 4 to 12) for years. Being pro-life and pro-family, I believe that service to families facing crisis pregnancies was vital. One of my greatest joys was serving on the board of Birthright and working as a birthing coach.

Through the years, I have mentored and mothered women in our church, our community, and even abroad. I am thrilled to have "adopted" daughters in Australia, the Dominican Republic, and Africa. My heart has always been for travel and missionary work. In my 40s, I traveled to Bosnia towards the end of the war, to bring humanitarian relief to bombed-out cities and villages. During our marriage, we travel yearly to Mexico, where we build homes, feed the poor, and minister to orphans.

Through all these ministry "assignments," I have experienced the love and provision of our Father first-hand. Through prophetic prayer and meditation, the Father creates a pathway for ministry that I never could have planned. He anoints all whom He appoints. He is just looking for people whose hearts are sold out to the Kingdom. He is looking for our availability and our "yes."

Writing this book has been both a joy and a challenge. I've co-authored two books on lighthouses with my husband. I've also written a children's book, which I plan to publish. I have had several careers, all of which entailed some form of writing. My passion for writing was nurtured at a young age by my dad, Stephen, who was a former high-school English teacher and a sportswriter for the *Cleveland Plain Dealer* and the *Cleveland Press*.

I believe that writing allows me to articulate my thoughts in unmatched ways. Spiritual writing is deeply personal. It's a conversation between God and me. Sometimes I hear His voice so clearly. Other times, I have to sit or walk in His presence until He speaks. I hope that this collection of conversations blesses you. I pray that everyone reading this will begin to have intimate conversations with the Father. Just remember, the biggest part of the conversation is listening.

DO YOU WANT TO BELONG TO GOD'S FAMILY?

Some of you who are reading this book may not have a relationship with God. Maybe you did at one time, but you have lost touch with the Father. Some may long to belong to God's family but don't know how to make that happen.

Others may think, "I want a relationship with the Father like Terri has." Well friends, it is possible today! Simply say this prayer:

Dear Father,

I admit that I have messed up. I am sorry for all of my sins. I believe in your son, Jesus, who paid the price for my sins by dying on the cross. I give my heart to You today. Please accept me into your family.

Amen

If you said this prayer, you just made the biggest decision of your life. I would love to send you some information and pray with you. Please reach out to me: Terri.tuers@yahoo.com May the Father bless you with His infinite love, wisdom, peace, and joy!

www.ingramcontent.com/pod-product-compliance
Ingram Content Group UK Ltd.
Pitfield, Milton Keynes, MK11 3LW, UK
UKHW020423250726
13967UKWH00007B/2793

9 781716 466762